*Only
with
Passion*

KATARINA WITT

WITH E. M. SWIFT

Only with Passion

Figure Skating's

Most Winning Champion

on Competition and Life

PublicAffairs

New York

Published in the United States by PublicAffairs™,
a member of the Perseus Books Group.

BOOK DESIGN BY JANE RAESE
Set in 11-point Berthold Bodoni

Library of Congress Cataloging-in-Publication Data
Witt, Katarina, 1965–
Only with passion : figure skating's most winning champion on competition
and life / by Katarina Witt with E. M. Swift. – 1st ed.
p. cm.
ISBN-13 978-1-58648-274-9
ISBN-10 1-58648-274-2
1. Witt, Katarina, 1965– . 2. Figure skaters—Germany—Biography.
3. Women figure skaters—Germany—Biography.
I. Swift, E. M. (Edward McKelvy) II. Title.
GV850.W58A3 2005
796.91'2'092—dc22
[B]
2005050944

FIRST EDITION
2 4 6 8 10 9 7 5 3 1

TO MY BELOVED MOM AND DAD

CONTENTS

Contents

ACKNOWLEDGMENTS

First, I would like to thank my best friend, Uwe Kästner, who introduced me to Sarah McNally—who spoke so fast that I wished she would write it down so I could understand her! She initiated the conversation about the book and helped make it happen. Thank you so, so much.

Ed Swift, thanks for your masculine interpretation of my feminine point of view. You did an amazing job and I hope your wife will forgive me for all the time you devoted to the book. She will love me forever for the Coffeemaker! It was great fun to host you in my hometown of Berlin.

Thanks to Frau Jutta Müller, my lifelong coach and mentor. You are one of the most passionate women I have ever met; every critique you gave I took as a compliment. I don't regret a moment.

Elisabeth Gottmann, you are the best. Your support and your strength make our business relationship strong, but more importantly, your understanding of every part of life and your warmth make our friendship so special. You are my dearest partner in crime.

Thanks to everyone at PublicAffairs for believing in my "Passion."

Jasmine , I will miss you . . .

Katarina Witt

This book would not have been born without the initiative of Sarah McNally. She was the architect of the collaboration and is a friend to book lovers everywhere.

I'd like to thank our editor, Lisa Kaufman, whose thoughtful suggestions breathed life into Jasmine's lungs.

I'm grateful to Katarina, whom I've long admired as a great skating champion, for her warmth, creativity, and trust.

And, while on the subject of strong, passionate women, I'd like to acknowledge the contributions of my mother, Joan McKelvy Taft, for giving me an enduring appreciation of the pleasures of dealing with the same.

E. M. Swift

PROLOGUE

This is the question I'm most frequently asked by people, especially young women: Katarina, how do you balance being an athlete and a woman?

"I am all the time a woman," is what I say.

Being a woman is not about balance, it's about discovery. Who am I? What do I want to be? Am I talented and committed enough to reach the goals I've set for myself?

Balance has nothing to do with finding the answers to these questions. The search for balance can lead to compromise, and no woman who's an athlete should feel compromised. I would never have been able to win two Olympic gold medals in figure skating in 1984 and 1988 if I'd been willing to compromise my core beliefs. So how do you balance being an athlete and a woman? Understand who you are and be true to yourself. That's how.

How do you categorize being a woman? Someone who's

weak? Someone who's tiny? Someone who's crying? Someone who's helpless without a man in her life? Or are you still a woman if you're strong, independent, self-reliant, and strong-willed? Both kinds are women, but they are different types.

I can be very feminine, but I can be masculine as well. Every person has both sides in them. A man has a feminine side, and a woman has a masculine side. Kurt Browning was once doing commentary for a professional competition in which I skated well. He said on the air: "If Katarina were a guy, I'd say, 'She's got balls.'"

The memory of that makes me smile. I'm proud of it. The life I live, my independence, the choices I've made and continue to make—these are areas traditionally considered masculine. I've never married. I support myself. I've never expected a man to look after me. At the same time, I know everyone perceives me as a woman. Men find me attractive, and I'm attracted to men. I'm very emotional, like a woman. When something goes wrong, I can burst into tears. I appreciate it when a man takes care of me. And I can easily imagine getting married if the right man comes into my life.

I find nothing contradictory in any of that. I am my own person. I never had a role model, exactly, but certainly I was a product of the environment in which I was raised. In the German Democratic Republic, which used to be called East Germany by most Westerners, there were never any negative connotations about being a woman athlete. When the Berlin Wall came down and relations opened with the West, I found out that other cultures had very different ideas about women in sports. In our system, we grew up believing, and seeing, that men and women were equal. Totally equal. Women did the same jobs as men in many fields, and they got paid the same for the work. Discrimination against women in the workplace was a totally new discussion for me. It never crossed my mind, or any of my girlfriends' minds, to marry a man in order to be taken care of, or in order to feel safe. We took care of ourselves. My mom worked. My aunt worked. Every woman I knew worked. And they raised their children without nannies. They were able to do it all.

I, too, have tried to do it all. My skating career has been so demanding I haven't been able to "balance" it with marriage and a family yet, as some skaters such as Kristi Yamaguchi, Nancy Kerrigan, and Katia (Ekaterina) Gordeeva have. But it's still possible that lies ahead. I'm preparing for a life after skating and look forward to that chapter in my life. The last two seasons were the first time in fifteen years I didn't spend the winter on a skating tour. It was strange to have so much time to myself, but I enjoyed it. It was nice to be home in Berlin, to be able to do things I hadn't done in years. I was able to accept invitations to award shows and fashion shows and other special events. I was able to attend the Berlin movie festival and to go skiing for a few days in Beaver Creek, Colorado, and Sun Valley, Idaho, stunningly beautiful places. I'm not a party girl, but to be able to go to the really nice festivities, to have a life away from bus rides and arenas and strange hotels that have been so much a part of my adult life—that was a wonderful change. Ever since 1988, after winning a second consecutive Olympic gold medal in Calgary, I'd spent every winter in the grip of a life on the road.

The break also gave me time to think about my future, to dream up and pursue my own creative projects. I'm not the kind of woman who just waits for someone to come to me with an offer. That's not me. I believe that sometimes you have to just go for it, to take the leap. So I toss a bunch of balls in the air, and though it's almost certain some of them will escape my grasp, perhaps even all of them, chances are I'll catch several. I like to be the one in charge. That means, however, instead of just skating in a pretty costume, I have to get TV deals in place, find sponsorships, assemble casts, hire choreographers, choose costumes, stage concepts, and help come up with music for the productions. For each of the past six years, I've headlined my own shows for NBC, four consecutive *Divas on Ice,* and two specials, *Katarina and Friends,* which feature individual and group performances by former Olympians skating before a live audience. I was privileged to work with some of the greatest skaters and musical performers in the world: Kristi Yamaguchi, Ekaterina Gordeeva, Nancy Kerrigan, Oksana Baiul, Steven Cousins, Diana Krall, Jessica Simpson, Renee Fleming, and Patti LaBelle.

All of this has made me very proud and has satisfied me as an artist, but it's also stressful. My life's a daily scramble. But I'm still pursuing my passions, which helps keeps me young. People have been asking me for more than twenty years, ever since I won my first Olympic gold medal in Sarajevo in 1984: What do you see yourself doing ten years from now? Could I make it to the next Olympics? (I didn't think so at the time.) How long do you think you can skate? In my wildest dreams I never thought I'd still be performing for audiences at the age of thirty-nine. You have five or six good years left, I thought when I was in my early twenties. Better make the most of it. Save your money, protect your image, plan for the future. As it turned out I just kept getting busier and busier every year. It was very strange, actually. What do I see myself doing ten years from now? I still can't answer this question. The truth is I've never wanted to answer it.

My response has always been the same. I'll take it year to year. Then I'll decide. I can remember times when I thought, "Two more years, then I'll retire. I'll leave skating behind." For twenty years I've been thinking that. More recently, I've been taking it one season to the next. Fall to winter to spring. Perhaps I should start thinking farther ahead, but I don't think I will change. Other people—for instance, my manager, Elisabeth Gottmann—can look ahead for me. I'm a woman who goes from season to season, and that's the way I follow my passions. I've never developed a long-term plan or strategy, and that's seemed to work for me so far.

I know that nothing I do in my future will be as exciting, as interesting, as fulfilling as my career in skating. The passion I have for skating will be challenging to duplicate. Performing for an audience . . . it's intoxicating. It's rewarding in a way that can't be duplicated anywhere else. When I talk to other athletes, they all say the same thing: Keep going as long as you can. Because after you've retired, everything will be different. You'll no longer be the one in the arena getting the attention. You have to be sure you're ready to finish that chapter of your life. If you stop too early, someday you'll regret it. You have to get to the point where you believe it's not worth it anymore. All the pain and effort to get in shape—not worth it. Bring on retirement. When that time comes, I'll know it. That's when I'll happily say, "Farewell."

I'm lucky, of course. Figure skating is an art form, an entertainment form. It's not just about competition, where people come to see you win or lose. That's what makes it so difficult to decide when to let go, because it's not like an athlete who can't win anymore, who's taking the place of a younger player who could help the team. It's just me and the performance, and the audience's reaction to it. I hope I don't get to the point where people watch me skate and think: "Oh my God, Katarina's not getting any speed out there. We'll have to push her around the ice." I don't want to be out there if I'm just a lovely ornament on skates.

But, who knows? When Dorothy Hamill was on the Tom Collins Tour of World and Olympic Champions nearing her late forties, I was amazed at how people still loved her. She skated with such warmth and style, her edging still flawless, so beautiful, and she seemed to love being out in the spotlight. American audiences are much more receptive than European audiences in that respect. They're much more loyal to the stars they've supported and followed. In Europe it's more the attitude: "Does she really need to be out there still? How sad." It's a different mentality.

My two winters away from touring also gave me time to work on this book. Within it are thoughts I'd have liked to express to a daughter or a younger sister about skating, competition, and life. It's such a different world today than when I was a child. Twenty years ago, early in my career, someone like me who was single, thirty-nine, childless, living alone, and working as an athlete would have been dismissed as a woman who only cared about work and perhaps was deficient emotionally. But today a lot of women live that way without feeling guilty about it, without feeling they're missing out on life. Yes, I love to work. But I love other things, too. I love intimacy. I love dining out with friends. I love spending time with my parents. I love fresh flowers and Berlin. I am still a whole person, a whole woman.

Yet today so often you hear how young women feel they have to choose—between catering to a boyfriend's interests and pursuing personal growth, between being nurturing and caring and being a competitive athlete, between being feminine and being strong and self-reliant, between being popular and being self-centered in order to reach high personal goals.

One such young woman, whom I shall call Jasmine Kronheim, spent a few days with me this spring, and during her stay we discussed these, and many more things. In the pages that follow, I have done my best to re-create that stay. Jasmine isn't her real name, nor is she a real person, but rather a composite of several young people I know. Her questions, however, are real. Her concerns are real. The journey before her is real. And in the process of writing this book, Jasmine's certainly become real to me.

No other names in this book have been changed, and to the best of my ability, everything else herein is factual and historically accurate.

*Only
with
Passion*

1

A Call for Help

"*I need your help,*" a familiar voice said over the phone.

It was my manager, Elisabeth Gottmann. This was a twist, since usually I'm the one who calls Elisabeth for help. She's much more than a manager: She's my business partner, my confidante, my friend. We own a sports and entertainment company together, and when I get an idea, she's the one I call to make it happen. I'm the one dreaming up schemes and projects, the creative artist. Elizabeth is the smart, practical businesswoman. How are we going to find the financing? Who can we get for a sponsor? How much will it cost? Where's the venue? Elizabeth has a tough reputation in business, because she's fiercely protective of me. But she's also honest and fair. We make a good team.

"How can I help you?" I asked, very cool, very professional, as if I were a concierge with all the answers.

"I need you to talk to a friend of mine," she said. "Actually, the daughter of a friend of mine. A skater. Her name's Jasmine. Jasmine Kronheim."

"What's this about?"

"Skating. Life. Coming of age. It's serious."

"That is serious. When does a girl come of age these days?"

"Good question. I have an eight-year-old. She's not there yet. Close. But I still have a year or two to go, I think. Jasmine's sixteen. Quite precocious. She and her mom are not seeing eye to eye on things at the moment about the future of her skating. So I volunteered you as an independent consultant. A mediator, if you will."

"Because I have all this time on my hands."

She laughed. She knew my schedule. It was, as usual, crammed. "You'll like this girl, I promise. She's very independent and disarming. You may even have seen her skate when you were doing your commentating on German TV. She trains with Peter Meier."

"*My* Peter Meier? From Chemnitz?" He'd coached me when I was a little girl, six and seven years old. He had to be in his sixties by now.

"He's in Dortmund now," Elisabeth said. "That's where Jasmine's from. He thinks she could be a great skater, maybe even a champion. She has all the talent in the world. But she's outgrown the Dortmund program, and he thinks she should go train at a place where she's around better skaters. To the States—a place like Lake Arrowhead. Or maybe Simsbury, Connecticut. He wants her to see if she can get to the next level. I remembered you telling me how much it helped when you were young to train every day with skaters who were better than you."

"And the girl?"

"Doesn't want to go. But for the wrong reasons."

"Meaning?"

"A boyfriend. Well, ostensibly a boyfriend. He may just be a cover for deeper issues: fear, self-doubt, questions of identity and rebellion."

Now it was my turn to laugh. This was beginning to sound familiar.

"And the joke is what exactly?" Elisabeth asked.

"It's just that some things never change."

"Right. Like your own history of teenage rebellion? That's occurred to me, too. So you'll help?"

"I'm so busy right now. You know how busy I am."

"I knew I could count on you."

"You're a pushy negotiator. Has anyone ever told you that?"

"Never."

"If, hypothetically, I accept this assignment, when would she like to talk?"

"I didn't say she wanted to talk. Her mother wants her to talk. She's one of my oldest friends, Kat. The sooner the better. Today, if possible."

"Not today."

"Then tomorrow. She's planning to visit Berlin anyway. She has friends in the city, but I already suggested you could put her up for a few days. I know your schedule, and you can fit her in."

"But tomorrow? So soon? I have the appointment with the sound studio to edit the music for the new show—"

"That's this afternoon."

"And I have to train. Frau Müller is coming—"

Elisabeth could hear the panic in my voice. "Perfect. Take her with you. You don't have guests, do you?"

"No, but . . . Oh, Elisabeth, you're impossible."

"I wouldn't ask this of anyone else. This came up quite suddenly, and her mother's in a panic. Jasmine's told her she wants to stay in Dortmund. She's threatened to leave school and move in with her boyfriend, who's a bartender. She'll give up skating and work as a waitress, if necessary. At sixteen! Call Peter Meier. The girl's got talent. He doesn't want her to waste it. Her mother can't talk to her about it anymore, and the father—don't get me started on him. Moved out two years ago and doesn't see why he should help pay for her lessons anymore. He won't even sign the divorce papers. A disaster. Forget him. Jasmine needs to hear from someone besides her mom, and I happen to know she's always looked up to you as a role model. The thoroughly modern woman: independent, athletic, but still, you know, attractive to men."

"What about you? You're attractive to men."

"Not in her eyes. I'm a neuter. An ancient. Worse than that: a mom. And no one ever asked me to pose in *Playboy*, which is a pretty cool thing to a girl like Jasmine. Besides, you're the one who skates. That's the thing about it: She loves skating. She loves to compete. Just like you. She didn't start skating until she was six, so she's still catching up with those little girls whose mothers pushed them out there as four-year-olds. But her learning curve is very steep. She has all the triple jumps and so much potential."

This was beginning to sound interesting. I could still remember what it was like to be a strong and willful teenager defying the wishes of my parents because of a boy. I could relate to young Jasmine.

"Are you sure about this?" I asked. "You may not like what I tell her. I'm not a mother."

"That's the point," Elisabeth said. "That's why she'll listen. Better it be to you than to one of her friends."

"All right. Tell her I have some things planned this week, but she can stay as long as she wants. Let me know what train she's on. I'll try to meet her."

"She has your address. She can walk."

"I'm just five minutes from the train station."

"I know. She'll manage. Thanks, Kat. For everything. I'll let you know when to expect her. This is just what she needs."

"We'll see. She's not going to be one of these sullen, vapid teenagers? She does have personality, right?"

"Bucketsful."

"I'll call you after she's settled."

"Love you, dear. Good luck."

It had been a long time since I'd thought about what it was like to be sixteen. Life changes so quickly at that age. I became European champion at seventeen, and Olympic champion at eighteen, winning my first gold medal in Sarajevo in 1984. A few months later, at the annual youth festival of the German Democratic Republic, I met my first boyfriend, Ingo, a drummer in a rock band. Though he looked young, he was twenty-five, seven years older than me, which is a huge gap at that age. His band was performing at the youth festival, and so was I. The lead singer was having a cup of coffee with me backstage, and I thought, "Hmm, he's kind of cute." He was interested in me, too. But then Ingo came up, and he was much younger and cuter than the singer. He had a little, tiny nose, which I always made fun of. And the brightest blue eyes. I fell for the drummer.

Ingo was such a sweet boy. Up until then I'd only spent time with other athletes, guys who treated me as a friend, a tomboy. Now for the very first time, here was a boy who made me feel like a girl, who brought me flowers. And he was a musician! I was really intrigued by him. Unannounced, he'd make the four-hour drive from Berlin to Chemnitz, where I trained, to pick me up after practice. That was so new to me. He was the opposite of an athlete: soft and gentle, not really a manly type. No big muscles. Very skinny. But I liked that. He had long dark-blonde hair and wore adventurous clothing, like bold, striped pants. He stayed out late and smoked cigarettes. The sportsmen I knew were more clean-cut. They had short hair, went to bed early, and for the most part, lived a disciplined life. What a difference! And on top of all that, Ingo was very much a gentleman in the way he treated me. Completely. Which is not the way you think of a musician in a rock band. That really flattered me. I fell in love with him despite the difference in our ages.

When he visited me, however, my parents were very strict. They didn't accept him and wouldn't let him stay at our home. So Ingo and I had to take a hotel room every time he visited, and he finally decided: I don't need this. Not at twenty-five. That's when I realized I needed my own apartment. I didn't want to lose Ingo, and I needed to start having my own life.

Eighteen, and wanting to live in my own apartment. It seems so young now. But the world I grew up in was so very different than it is today. I was an elite athlete, which was of high importance in the GDR. I had a handler who was responsible for making sure I could concentrate on my sport, that I suffered as few distractions as possible. This person was not a coach but was more like a supervisor, a facilitator. Someone well connected I could go to if I had a problem. It was this person I asked about getting my own apartment, which was a special privilege in East Germany, and I was told if I won another European championship—I'd won my first in 1983—then an apartment would become available. And that became my goal.

As promised, when I became European champion again the next winter, I got my apartment. It was a tiny one-bedroom with a kitchen and a bathroom. The entire place was the size of my kitchen today. It was in Chemnitz, just a five-minute drive from the apartment I lived in with my parents. And it wasn't as if they just gave it to me. I paid rent for it. But I had money from the government for winning the Olympics. In this hidden way, all the East German athletes were really professionals. But the authorities always had a hand on the money. It was kept in an account controlled by your handler, and when you wanted it, you had to ask for it. If you'd been doing well, you'd get it. If not, maybe you wouldn't.

My parents didn't know about the apartment, and I couldn't bring myself to tell them. I kept living at home, slowly fixing up my new place without their knowledge. My mom, Kate, worked as a physical therapist. My dad, Manfred, sold seeds to farmers. They worked hard. But the secret finally came out when I left for Tokyo to defend my World Championship title in March 1985.

In East Germany, the residents were responsible for cleaning the hallway floors of their apartment buildings. One person organized the schedule, and the tenants traded off in a rotation. While I was away at the World Championships, the scheduler in my building visited my parents wanting to know who'd be responsible for cleaning when my turn in the rotation came. Of course this was news to them, and not pleasant news. That's how they found out I was preparing to move out of their home.

When I flew home from Tokyo, they came to the airport to meet me. Even though I'd won the World Championships, they were very quiet, which was unusual and awkward. My father told me what had happened, about the man coming by to discuss the cleaning. He said neither he nor my mom would have anything to do with my new apartment. I'd have to organize everything: the furnishing, the painting, the cleaning, the maintenance. My parents wouldn't lift a finger. My dad wouldn't so much as pound a nail into the wall for me. It was so unlike him. Clearly, they were hurt that I wanted to leave, but I'd made up my mind and wasn't going to back down. I didn't want to make them upset, but moving out of their apartment was the only way I could move forward with my own life. Eventually they'd understand that. It took a very long time before I had the apartment fixed up enough to move in, because of the hours and hours of training I had to put in every day. But members of my sports club pitched in, and six months later I was living on my own.

It was then that I learned a valuable lesson: You can rebel from your parents without losing them. Although we had a very strained relationship during that period, I knew that my parents still loved me. They were still my parents. I didn't want to lose them. So I kept the communication lines open. I'd come home and sit and talk with them. Finally, after some months of this tension, my mother said, "Okay, bring me your laundry. You're busy. I'll do it for you." That's when I knew everything was going to be fine.

I ended up having a much better relationship with my parents than I'd had before. When I was living with them, I left the house in the morning in time to make a 7 A.M. practice and wouldn't get home until 6 P.M. I'd be exhausted. We'd have dinner together, watch TV, then go to bed. It was always the same. We never talked about things. I didn't want to talk to them anyway, because I was in those teenage years when I only wanted to do things my own way.

Once I moved out, however, once I had my own space, I became more of a visitor at their home. That was nice because we made time for each other, instead of wasting our time. We started to talk in a way we hadn't when I lived there. My relationship with them became much closer than it had ever been before. I'd visit even if I didn't have laundry to do. In a way, they won me back, because now we were spending more quality time together. I still had my freedom, my own space, my own life. For everyone, I think, it turned out better.

I wondered if something like that was happening between Jasmine and her mother. It sounded as if Elisabeth's friend's daughter was at the stage where she only wanted to do things her own way. When you're a teenager and have a serious boyfriend, all you really want to do is spend every second with him. Stay out late at night. That isn't good for an athlete in training. It used to drive my coach, Frau Jutta Müller, crazy. It was even harder on her than on my parents. But for me, even after I met Ingo, skating was always the top priority. I never lost sight of that. I knew where my future lay. I was curious to find out if Jasmine felt the same way.

2

Jasmine

The following morning I placed a call to Peter Meier. It had been several years since we'd talked, but we knew each other well and were immediately comfortable with one another over the phone. We briefly caught up with what had been going on with our lives, then I asked him about Jasmine. It was as Elisabeth had said. She had talent that he didn't want to see her waste. She'd outgrown him and, especially, had outgrown her peers in Germany, which wasn't producing many world-class skaters. He thought it was important she begin training every day with the best, pushing herself, measuring herself against those she would one day need to beat. Jasmine had come late to skating, but she was a tremendous natural athlete with an urge to compete. He wasn't sure if she had a champion's tempera-ment, however. She could be lazy about training and seemed satisfied just to get to the podium. Second place? Third place? It seemed all the same to her. He thought it had a lot to do with the attitude of her father, who'd never taken her skating very seriously. It was a hobby to outgrow, like riding ponies. The mother's expectations were considerably higher, but Jasmine was far more interested in the attention of her father. Mr. Meier believed Jasmine needed to commit to skating if she was going to move up the ladder internationally, to really give it her all; otherwise she was just wasting everyone's time and money.

It was midafternoon when the buzzer in the hallway startled me at my desk. Someone was ringing from the street. I pressed the intercom button. "Hello?"

"Miss Witt? It's Jasmine Kronheim."

"Jasmine! I'm on the fourth floor, all the way to the top. I'll buzz you in."

I waited for my young houseguest at the landing. Her footsteps echoed up the stairwell, and I could tell she was taking the steps two at a time. I live in an old building in what had been the East German sector of the city. It had been recently renovated—new plumbing, wiring, floors, and paint—and I had the top floor. From my tiny rooftop garden I had a view of the city, which I loved. My parents lived in the apartment two floors below me—ironic, yes? A childhood friend, Uwe Kästner, whose mother had been a doctor at my sports club, leased the apartment directly below mine. So this, to me, is home, with a strong connection to my past.

"The walk up keeps me in shape," I said as Jasmine came into view.

"No doubt," she said with a bright smile. She was quite a beautiful girl. Her hair was short, light brown, worn in a casually stylish way. It was a sophisticated cut, making her look older than sixteen. Her body looked older, too. She was wearing jeans and had a nice figure and an athletic way of moving, confident and fluid. She was slender and about my height, five feet six, which is tall for a figure skater. Like so many kids in Berlin, Jasmine's T-shirt was too short to cover her waist, leaving her midriff bare despite the chill in the air outside. I had to bite my tongue to stop myself from telling her she was underdressed. The best way to develop back problems is to walk around in the cold like that. And if she wanted to skate, she didn't want back problems. I took her hand and kissed her on both cheeks. "Welcome to my home."

"This is a very cool neighborhood," she said.

"Do you think so? I love it. Berlin Mitte, it's called—Middle Berlin. It used to be in the Eastern sector."

"What's the big dome down the street?"

"This way? The New Synagogue. This whole area was the Jewish quarter during the war. It's now full of artists and students, very young, very hip. You'll fit right in. But I must warn you, the red-light district is just down the street. I hope you weren't solicited on the way."

"Not today."

"Humboldt University is just a ten-minute walk. There are lots of clubs nearby and wonderful restaurants and shops. I'll give you the tour tomorrow if you like."

She shrugged. She was carrying a small backpack, which she let drop in the hall. "Don't worry about me," Jasmine said. "I'm okay poking around by myself. I promised my mom I'd spend tonight with you, then I've got some friends I'm going to look up. I don't want to be any trouble."

"You're no trouble at all. I have three bedrooms here. We don't even have to see each other. I'll give you a spare key."

She was moving through the apartment as we talked and had found the kitchen. "This is twice as big as our kitchen," she said. "What's this?" Jasmine had found my new cappuccino maker. "Oh . . . my . . . God. Does it work?"

"Yes? Would you like a cup of cappuccino?"

She opened a couple of cabinets. "I haven't had a thing to eat or drink since breakfast. How do you work it?" she asked, returning to the cappuccino machine. She was making herself right at home.

"Hands off my new toy," I said. "It's Swiss. If you push the wrong button it might vacuum the floor."

"Oh." She smiled at my joke. "Note to self: Beware of appliances made by little Swiss cappuccino elves."

"How would you like it? Whipped milk and sugar?"

"Please."

Jasmine opened the door of the refrigerator and poked her head inside. She came out with a square of cheesecake. "May I?" she asked, barely waiting for an answer.

"Of course. My father made it. It's incredible, no?"

"Hmm. My God, yes. How do you stay so thin with things like this in the fridge?"

"Have as much as you like," I said with a smile. "That way it won't end up on my hips."

"I promise I won't devour you out of house and home. I'm just staying tonight."

"As you wish."

"My mom wants me to talk to you about the situation I'm in, so that's what I'm doing here. Then I'm gone."

"So you said." I handed her the cappuccino and started to make one for myself. The machine ground and whirred and steamed with Swiss efficiency. "Chocolate?" I offered, setting an assorted box of German chocolates on the kitchen table. Jasmine was prowling like an animal and I wanted to get her settled in one place.

My young friend sat down and eyed the chocolates carefully. Finally she took one covered in dark chocolate. She took a bite, made a tiny face of disapproval, and set the remainder down on the napkin I'd set before her. Then she chose another chocolate, this one covered in white. It apparently was to her liking, because she finished it in two bites. The other remained on the napkin.

"A situation?" I asked as innocently as I was able. "Not desperate, I hope."

She rolled her eyes. "Oh, it's so not worth talking about," she began.

"But as long as you're here . . . since you promised."

For the next half hour Jasmine spoke, the words coming hesitantly at first, punctuated by embarrassed laughs and arching eyebrows. Then, slowly, she became more comfortable talking about herself, egged on by my gentle words of encouragement. Her words were flowing steadily now, like a stream, tumbling from one subject to the next. I mostly listened, nodding, smiling when she smiled, patient. It made me remember what it was like to be young, to have your future before you, to be faced with a dizzying maze of possibilities while armed only with the power of youth and a fragile belief in your own capabilities and judgment.

Jasmine was apparently a good skater and athlete. What I couldn't tell, even as she spoke, was whether she was a serious skater and athlete. She just didn't seem emotionally involved in her options, except when she was discussing her boyfriend.

"So tell me more about him. What's his name?"

"Bernard. Like a St. Bernard? That's what he reminds me of, a big sweet St. Bernard puppy. St. Bernie, I call him, which drives him crazy, but I can just see him with one of those little casks strapped around his neck, digging through the snow to save someone, his big soft sad brown eyes . . ." She giggled madly. "He works as a bartender in Dortmund, which sends my mother off the deep end. But he's ambitious. He's not just going to be drawing liters of lager the rest of his life, you know? He's saving up and wants to open his own club. He's already got a business partner scouting for locations."

"He sounds like he's got his life all mapped out."

"Oh, he does. I mean, he's always thinking ahead. He's amazing."

"And where do you fit into his long-range plans?"

"Jesus, I don't know. I mean, I've only known him a month. A little more, I guess. Actually it's our five-week anniversary today."

"And he's how old?"

She rolled her eyes. "Twenty-four. And I'm only sixteen. I've heard it all before, so don't start."

"I'm not starting anything. I'm just trying to get the lay of the land. And have you had other serious boyfriends, or is Bernard your first?"

"I've had boyfriends before, but I guess you could say this is my first real relationship. My mother disapproves, if you haven't picked that up. I don't care. He's the best thing to happen to me. He makes me happy in a way no one has before. I feel, I don't know, not adult, but not like a kid. I mean, I know I'm young to be seeing a guy his age, but it feels right, you know? It just does. I can't explain it."

"And how does all this affect your skating?"

"My coach, Mr. Meier—you had him, right?"

"I did. As a young girl."

"He told my mom that if I wanted to reach my potential, I should think about going to the States to train with better skaters."

"He's probably right about that, unfortunately."

"Well, I'm not sure that's such a great idea."

"I see. And why is that, just so I'm clear on your reasons."

She was hesitant, shrugging her shoulders. "I don't want to move away."

"Are you worried about losing your boyfriend?"

"Well, of course. I mean, he's really cute, and the other girls at the bar all flirt with him like mad. If I went to the States, there's no way we'd survive. I'm not ready for that, you know?" She shrugged again.

"And how do you feel about skating? About competing?"

"Oh, I love all that. I really do. I just don't know if I'm good enough to, you know, pursue it the way Coach Meier wants me to. I'd like to train with those other top girls. I think he's right. It would make me work harder and all. And California would be a really cool place to hang for a while. Lake Arrowhead, right? Have you been there?"

"Yes. Many times. It's lovely. It's in the mountains, not far from L.A. Lots of other young skaters around. I think you'd find it very stimulating."

"My English isn't that good. I've taken it in school and all, but outside of ordering food and maybe asking directions, I could never have a real conversation. It'd be hard to make friends."

"I wouldn't worry too much about that. You'd pick it up soon enough. The real question you have to ask yourself is how serious you are about becoming a great skater. Or at least the best you can be. Maybe good enough to make it to the Olympics. It takes a lot."

"I know that. I mean, I'd kill to go to the Olympics. I would. I'd kill. My mother's been talking about that since I was, I don't know, about ten. But it's not her life, you know? It's mine."

"I totally agree."

"I'm curious whether I could be good enough one day," she said. "I guess that's the main reason I'm here. I don't want to give up Bernard, and I don't want to give up my skating. I'm at the proverbial crossroads of my life, as they say."

"It's not enough to be curious. You have to commit 110 percent in order to find out how good you can be, or you're doomed to fail. You can't just wonder."

"I know that. I do. But I don't want to live my life lost in some fantasy of my mother's. I mean, you know the odds of succeeding. They're like a zillion to one."

"I talked to Mr. Meier this morning. He thinks you have the talent. But he wasn't sure whether you have the ambition and work ethic."

"He said that?"

"In so many words. And if you have talent—and trust me, Jasmine, a lot of girls have talent—then the difference between realizing a dream and losing yourself in a fantasy is hard work. It's that simple."

She thought about that without commenting. The longer we

talked, the more her original posturing softened. Jasmine had
had an attitude at the outset, an outward bravado that I felt certain was mostly an act. I liked listening to her, though. I liked
her beautiful innocence, her youthful belief that there is a right
path for every person, if only you can figure it out. You lose that
as you get older. You realize that all paths are similar if the same
person walks them. I live a similar life to the one I lived twenty-
three years ago, when I was Jasmine's age, and I still spend
much of my time with young people because of my skating. I
train, I get into shape, I practice, I perform, I travel. It's a life I
know well. Sometimes I feel I'm still back in school, because I'm
still playing my sport. I've grown up, certainly, but I'm on the
same path. I haven't changed careers. I haven't been on a
steady, evolutionary progression from school and study, to career, to family and kids, like other women my age. I've never
had that last responsibility. So it was nice for me to listen to Jasmine, to feel not like her mom, but like an older sister. As if I
was taking care of someone else. It was good.

"Well?" she finally asked.

"Well what?" I said, looking at her gently. "Do you expect
me, after talking to you for one hour, to tell you how to live your
life?"

She looked at me, uncertainty in her eyes.

"I'm not going to, my dear. It doesn't mean I'm not interested. And it doesn't mean I can't help. It just means it isn't so
simple as me telling you something and you walking out the
door tomorrow morning to go play with your friends."

She wasn't expecting this. She shrugged.

"Hungry? Do you like Italian?"

"Yes."

"Let's order some. There's an excellent Italian restaurant around the corner that delivers. We can't talk on an empty stomach now, can we? Well, I can't. Then I can take you on a little journey through the streets of my life. You might find it relevant."

"I'd like that. God, I'd love to hear about the Olympics."

"Good." I retrieved a menu from the drawer. "Here are your choices. If you like veal, I recommend the picata. And the lasagne's very good."

She looked at the menu for a minute then handed it back. "The veal picata sounds nice."

"A green salad to start?"

"Um . . . sure. Uh . . ." she was struggling to say something. "I'm not sure what to call you."

I laughed. "Call me Katarina."

"Okay," she said, blushing. "Good. Katarina. Do I have time for a shower? I'd love to freshen up from the trip."

"Come on. I'll show you your room."

3

The Skater in Me

I was on my second glass of wine, enjoying my last bite of veal, as Jasmine told me about when she'd competed at junior Nationals. "It was in Munich, and I was twelve years old, which was younger than most of the other junior girls. I'd qualified by coming in second at the regionals in Dortmund, which is a pretty pathetic district. So no one expected me to do anything in Munich. I'd missed Nationals as a novice with a sore ankle, so I was basically a total unknown. But I was so young I guess I wasn't nervous, because I absolutely nailed my long program and came in second overall. I was, like, blown away. I'd never once skated that program cleanly in practice. I was totally in shock, and all these flowers and stuffed animals came raining down, and I started picking them up like one of the flower girls. I was in this dirndl outfit, my hair in braids—very cute, very, I

don't know, saucy and little girlish. Coach Meier had totally designed my program and costume to appeal to the blue-haired
judges. And it worked. But, my God, what a feeling it was to
hear that applause! I didn't want to leave the ice. They had to,
like, push me off so the next skater could skate."

"There's nothing better. Trust me, it never gets old."

Her face was shining from the memory. "Of course, the next
year I got the other end of the stick, skating off as the audience
clapped sympathetically after I'd made a hash of my performance. I think they were worried I'd hurt myself. I finished, like,
seventh, and just wanted to crawl into a hole and cover myself
up with a burlap bag. Please, God, make me disappear."

"I've been there, too, I'm afraid."

"It's the pits. So this year, which was my first year in seniors, I
came in fourth, which was the goal my coach had set for me. So
we were pretty happy with the result. You were doing commentary for television."

I remembered her now. I'd been charmed by her appearance,
and though her technique on her jumps was a little ragged, I
thought she should have finished third. I told her so.

"You think so? You're great to say so, but I wasn't disappointed. Next year I will be if I don't make it to the podium. But
I was a little surprised to get fourth, to tell you the truth."

"You shouldn't have been. You have to have self-confidence,
Jasmine. If you don't believe in yourself, who will?"

"That's what my mom says. Of course, she never skated."

"Take it from me, you should have been third."

She smiled, inwardly delighted. Then she shrugged her
shoulders dismissively. "Enough about my small-potatoes hero-
ics. You were going to tell me about the Olympics."

"Was I?" I said, laughing. "But I enjoy listening to you!"

"I'm talked out. You're the champion. There's so much I want to hear about you. Tell me how you got your start. Was your mom a skater, or what?"

"By nagging and begging and pleading for months," I said, smiling at the memory. "I was five, maybe six years old. We lived in Chemnitz, which at that time was called Karl Marx Stadt. My mom worked in a hospital. That's where I went to kindergarten, in the hospital's day care center. Every day, during lunch break, we visited the ice rink in the woods. I always stopped and watched. The rink was cold, and wet, and dark, but I felt drawn to it. It was as if the skater in me was trying to get out. I can't explain it any other way. No one in my family was a skater. My older brother was a soccer player. My mother danced some, and my father was a singer when he was younger. They certainly had no intention for me to become an athlete, and it wasn't like I was dreaming of becoming an Olympic champion. But something about that rink called to me, and I bugged my parents to take me there. For half a year I begged them: 'Please let me skate. I want to be a skater.' They kept waiting for me to forget about it.

"Sports in East Germany were very well organized. They were always looking for young talent, young athletes, and there were ads in the papers telling families to bring their children to try out for skating. Finally, after months of listening to me complain, my mother gave in and took me to the rink.

"She's the one who remembers all this. For me, it's just a very distant memory. But the first time I went I was dressed in my street clothes, and there were already 100 skaters in my age group who'd been skating in that program for half a year. The ice surface was wet along the sides, but in the middle it was dry. So my mother told me: 'Go to the middle.' She didn't want me to fall and have to go home in wet clothes. So instead of creeping along the boards the way most kids did when they first stepped on ice, I skated to the middle without falling. The coach, an older man, said to my mom, 'I cannot promise you a world champion, but she can stay with the group, as long as in the next half year she catches up with the others.' And that's what I did. I learned what they had learned, and more, by the end of the year. After two or three years, I was the only one of those 100 children who was left."

"I don't understand," Jasmine said. "The others quit?"

"That was the way things were done in the sports schools. It was where all the most talented athletes in the country trained. Our first priority was sports, and then came school. We had to meet certain goals in order to be promoted to the next class. If you didn't meet the goals, you were told to leave. The very first competition I entered, in Dresden, I won. I was seven. In fact it was December 3, my seventh birthday. By the time I was nine, I could do all the double jumps, except the double axel. That was the year Frau Müller discovered me and took me into her group."

I wasn't going to bore Jasmine with all the details of my skating career, but the fact is, Frau Jutta Müller was the most successful figure-skating coach in East Germany. Maybe in the world. Overall her athletes won fifty-seven medals in European, World, and Olympic championships. She, too, lived in Karl Marx Stadt, which was my luck, because I didn't have to move away from home to have the finest coaching. But it was pretty scary at first. I was nine, and my sweet, even-tempered coach, Frau

Loucky, who had taken me into her group after I'd been with Peter Meier, sat me down and said: "Frau Müller has chosen you to be in her group." Any other skater would have been totally thrilled, but I burst into tears, because I knew, even at that young age, that now the fun times were over. I'd been skating in a group of four or five kids my age who were my closest friends. We had such a good time on and off the ice, and we did everything together. Now I had to leave and join Frau Müller's group, teenagers who were all five to eight years older than me. I'd seen her on the ice, and Frau Müller was loud, always screaming. She was a tough coach. I'd always hunch down lower when I saw her and try to hide.

At the same time I knew that Frau Müller only picked the best. Now I had a chance to be successful. And I must say the first year with her was really fun. She treated me like a child, gently and encouragingly, and taught me the double axel. She used to tell me, "You have so much talent. You can't waste it. I won't allow you to." So I was always thinking: "Katarina, you have to be successful." I loved skating purely from the viewpoint of being an athlete. Every day I was learning something new. Every day I was trying to move up the ladder.

When I turned eleven, though, things got a little more serious. Frau Müller's secret was to take the younger, talented skaters into an older group, so you were always around people who were better than you were. That's the best way to learn. I was now skating with Anett Pötzsch, who in 1980 would become Olympic champion and was five years older than me. She could do triples. Also a boy, Jan Hoffmann, who won a silver medal in the Lake Placid Olympics. He could do triples. They didn't like training with a little kid, but I was always the competitor. I always wanted to do better than everyone else. So those were the perfect surroundings for me.

Anett especially didn't appreciate me being in her group. By the time I was twelve, I could do the triple toe loop and triple salchow, and the competitiveness grew between us. That's what Frau Müller wanted, and in some ways it was good, because technically, Anett and I were on the same level. She started to be afraid of me, the up-and-comer, which was silly because at the international level, there was a whole generation of skaters between us. Anett was a woman and had great compulsory figures. I was, in relative terms, a baby. You had to work your way up in those years. It wasn't like later, after they got rid of compulsories and someone like Oksana Baiul could arrive on the scene and in one year win the World Championships and the Olympics. You had to pay your dues before the judges rewarded you with high placements. That was something I had to accept.

By the time I was fourteen, I could outskate Anett technically. She didn't like that, and instead of supporting me, she did everything she could to antagonize me. She never included me in their games or conversations, always treating me like a little kid who was in the way. She never told me anything encouraging. Later she married my brother, and we became good friends. But at the time we were skating together, she saw me as an enemy. That brought out my competitive side. Every day in practice I'd think: I'll show you today. I'll kick ass. I was a very arrogant little girl at that age, but it was a childish arrogance. I liked to pretend I was confident and self-assured, but I really wasn't. I just didn't want to take directions or advice from the older kids.

"What was she like?" Jasmine asked.

"Who?" I realized I'd been lost in thought and had completely lost the thread of our conversation.

"Frau Müller. Your coach."

"She was always an authority figure. She still is. I still work with her, you know. She's seventy-six. In fact I have a session with her tomorrow if you'd like to come watch."

"I would like that. I'd love that," Jasmine said, eyes bright.

"Good. It's in the morning. When I see Frau Müller today, I think: What a beautiful woman she still is. Wow. I'd love to be able to age like her. And when I look at the old pictures of us together, when she was much younger, I see what a strong, beautiful woman she was. But of course when I was your age, I was fearful of her. I respected her. At the same time I enjoyed being with her. We were perfect for each other, basically. She's a tiny woman, very fragile in appearance, and she always watched her weight. She was vain in that respect. If she gained a pound or two, she'd skip lunch. And it was the same if I gained a pound or two," I added, laughing. "Whatever she asked of an athlete, she asked of herself. We were under the same regimen. And she was very young somehow. Very energetic and determined. She worked as hard as we did. She's a Sagittarius, and I'm a Sagittarius. I knew we would fight each other every step of the way, but we'd get along. I was able to take Frau Müller's strength, her power, her meanness, even, and use it. There were skaters who broke under that, who couldn't deal with her. But not me. For me, it was perfect.

"She'd make me do a jump over and over and over, which I didn't want to do, of course, so I'd fight it. The triple flip, for instance, was my hardest jump, and one time she wouldn't let me leave the ice until I did it. It didn't matter if I landed on my ass after doing it, I had to do it." Jasmine laughed as I mimicked falling awkwardly. "That was a fight, let me tell you. I knew I could do the jump, but I didn't want to give her the satisfaction. I was getting madder and madder. I kept opening up during the rotations. I didn't think she'd dare make me stay on the ice for all that time and kept thinking she'd say, okay, we try again tomorrow. I didn't know then that she was stronger than me. The Zamboni machine was sitting there for half an hour, and she wouldn't let the driver clean the ice. She told him, 'No, you wait. Katarina has to do this jump.' After half an hour, I gave up. I did the triple, fell on my ass, and she calmly said, 'Okay, you can go now. Let's have lunch.' I tell you, Jasmine, she was a fantastic coach."

"She sounds tough. Tougher than Peter Meier. I wonder how I'd do under a tough coach like that."

"You need a push in the back sometimes. Whether you're an athlete or in some other walk in life, you can't always do it yourself. In sports, maybe 80 percent of your effort is your own free will, and the other 20 percent is pain. Torture. You need someone cracking the whip at you to reach your potential.

"My first boyfriend, Ingo, was a musician. He used to tell me I was so lucky to have Frau Müller pushing me. He regretted his mother hadn't pushed him when he was taking piano lessons as a boy, hadn't forced him to practice when he didn't want to. If she had, he'd have been a better musician. You can't do it all by yourself no matter how strong you think you are. Neither, of course, can the coach. In the end, a coach is only as good as her athlete. You can be an incredible coach, but it's your student who must prove it. So in a way the reputation of the coach is in the hands of the student. Frau Müller hated that. She hated when one of her students failed. There was always a little fear in her eyes. I see that now when I look at the old pictures, but at the time I never thought of her as vulnerable. I both trusted and feared her completely. She could have told me anything, and I'd have done it."

"Really? I've never trusted anyone that much in my life."

"It's true. I spent more time with Frau Müller than with my family. She had me my whole competitive career, since I was nine. You don't see that much anymore with skaters. There's not much loyalty left these days. It's sad. If you're not successful, or go through a bad patch, you move on. You think your coach failed. Some skaters are unwilling to take the blame on themselves. They point their finger somewhere else. I've been following Michelle Kwan's career the last few years, and very much admire what she's done for skating. But I thought it was really sad for her coach, Frank Carroll, when just before the 2002 Olympics, she fired him and decided to compete without a coach, after he'd brought her so far. So when she lost to Sarah Hughes in Salt Lake City—and this sounds really terrible to admit—I couldn't help thinking: What goes around, comes around. It was like the skating god decided Michelle had hurt someone badly, and now she'd be hurt, too. You wonder why she couldn't have just gone through that last season with him as a thank-you for all those years together."

I stopped and shrugged. Who knew? "Then again, you can never know what happened between them if you weren't there, and I wasn't there. She's an adult and obviously knew what she was doing. So really, I can't judge. A coach has to change through the years, too. If they take you when you're young, they have to accept it when you grow up. They have to accept that you'll have your own ideas, and let you be a partner, and not just a student. Frau Müller was good at that later in my career, and I don't know if that was the problem between Frank and Michelle, or not. But from the outside, where I sat, it didn't seem right, you know?"

Jasmine nodded. "When did you know you wanted to be, you know, a champion? Not just good. The best."

I smiled. "I remember it very clearly. I was fourteen. It was in 1980. I was watching Anett Pötzsch get her gold medal at Göteborg, Sweden, at the European Championships. I trained with her every day, and I knew if she could do it, I could do it. As I listened to the national anthem being played, I knew I wanted to stand on that podium one day, too. That's why Frau Müller was smart having me train with the older students. It put those thoughts in my head."

"So how long did it take?"

"Several more years. But I worked my way up year by year, steadily."

"Did you ever feel like quitting? After not winning, I mean? Did you ever come close to giving up on yourself?"

"Not at all. No. For me, the feeling was that I had to get to the top. And I knew I would. I just knew it. But I had to learn how to get there. If I finished third or fourth, I knew there was a reason. There was something I could fix. Or something I could have done in training that would have prevented it. When I was about your age, Jasmine, I was sometimes rebellious with Frau Müller. She'd tell me to do something, and I'd say, 'No.' Eventually I'd give in, of course, but I fought her all the time. I should have been world champion at seventeen. But in a way it was right that I failed, because I only worked in practice hard enough to get by. I put on weight in the summer, because the winter always seemed so far away. My athletic coach would tell me to go running, and I'd hide behind the trees with a friend and go to the bakery and eat cake for half an hour. Then we'd rub our cheeks to make them red and come back panting."

Jasmine cried with delight, "You did that? Oh . . . my . . . God!"

"Yes, but I always knew when to work hard again, to be serious about training. Still, I tried to do as much as possible by giving as little as possible, you know? And when I was seventeen, I did this more than usual. That's the year I came in fourth in the World Championships, after finishing second the year before in Copenhagen in 1982.

"That was the year of my biggest lesson in skating. I'll tell you this one story, and then we're going to bed. I was sixteen. I'd been fifth in the world in 1981, so I was already a skater the judges knew. My biggest threat was Elaine Zayak, an American girl. We both had a chance to win our first World Championship. I took my position on the ice before my free skating program started, and I started to feel afraid. I thought: 'You know what, I still have time to go to the referee and tell him I don't want to skate.' That's how afraid I was. Then I thought: 'If I am careful, I'll be okay. And that's the worst thought you can have as an athlete.' Then the music started, and I had to skate.

"I made a number of mistakes, because through the entire program I was cautious and afraid. I kept thinking: 'I hope I can do the triple jump. I hope I can do the combination. I hope this is going well.' So I ended up finishing second. The lesson I came away with was: Once you're out there, you have no choice. You have to deliver. You can't hesitate. You have to be aggressive.

You can't try to be careful: Go for it. Don't hesitate. Turn caution into aggression. Only when you attack are you able to deal with your nerves.

"That was the lesson of my life as a skater, and from then on I was always more aggressive in competition than I was in practice. We have a German expression for moments of greatest pressure: When you feel the fists in your neck. You know it, Jasmine? You know this feeling? Well, when I felt the fists in my neck, from that point on I was always at my best. Actually, that's why I began to enjoy skating last in a competition, because that's when the pressure was greatest."

She looked at me with open admiration. "How do you teach someone that? To be her best when the pressure is greatest. I'd love to do that."

"You can tell someone about it, but you can only learn how to do it from personal experience. Listen, you're always going to feel nervous. I was always nervous, but I was cool about it, because I knew what to do. That's why afterward in competitions some of the girls hated me. They knew I could do it. In practice, we were always four or five girls on the same level, more or less. But I knew I could deliver in a competition, and that's what set me apart. Even if I wasn't perfect, I delivered more than the other girls. You either have it or you don't. This is what sets a champion apart from other world-class athletes. There are lots of world-class skaters during practice. But the true champion is able to deliver when it counts. You're born with it, or you're not."

"Some skaters use sports psychologists."

"That's true. I never needed one. I tried it one time, and it was a disaster. I was about fourteen or fifteen, and she came in to hypnotize me: Your arms are heavy . . . your legs are heavy.

. . . Then she got me to visualize my jumps. Okay, so then I got onto the ice, and my arms still felt heavy. My legs still felt heavy. I felt blah." Jasmine laughed as I mimicked slumping around the ice. "I couldn't even jump two inches off the ice!"

"That's funny."

"Everybody's different. You have to find your own individual solution for dealing with pressure, and that's something a good coach can help you with. The worst thing is when a kid always does well in practice but knows when she goes into competition, she'll fall apart when it counts. It makes her try to do things differently, to change her routine, because the old way never worked in the past. You have to learn you can do it in competition exactly the way you do it in practice. But you have to deliver a few times before believing this. You have to break through the pattern of failure. That's what's hard. A lot of people are physically prepared for competition. The champions are the ones who are mentally prepared."

"And that was your strength."

"I think so, yes. Many people thought I was best at flirting with the judges, but I think it was my mental toughness. I could deliver when it counts."

"Cool."

"Yes, it was cool. Now, my dear, I must get my rest. And I hope you'll still be here in the morning."

4

The Coach

I rose early to make some phone calls. The first was to Elisabeth, to tell her Jasmine had arrived safely and that things seemed to be going along well. Then we moved on to some business matters we had to discuss, plus some interview requests that had come in, the details of a charity dinner the following week, and the summer plans of her daughter, Ellen. We could have talked all morning. As I said earlier, Elisabeth is much more than a business partner and manager to me—she's also my closest friend.

We met in 1990. It was a different world then. The Berlin Wall came down in November 1989, and the German Democratic Republic I grew up in became a memory. I was twenty-three, had won two Olympic gold medals, and was touring all over the United States. Elisabeth was in her late twenties, working as an assistant with a management firm in the music business. She was very smart, very energetic and attractive. It was an exciting period in German history, but also a confusing one. I'd been comfortable with my situation in the old GDR. The new freedoms that came with the fall of the wall also meant uncertainty. I didn't know how the changes were going to affect my life. No one thought about reunification at the time. We just thought there'd be a more democratic GDR. Everything was new, unsettled, in transition. I used to have to get the permission of the government if I wanted to travel or perform in a show or get an apartment. Suddenly I was the only one who had to decide what I wanted to do. And I wanted to do everything. To try everything. My brain whirled with the possibilities.

Elisabeth was from Frankfurt, the West, and she knew she could help me with these changes. I've been lucky in that I've always surrounded myself with talented people. I'm not someone who says: I can do everything myself. I know how far I can go on my own, and then I hire good people who help me bring my vision to life. I'm able to delegate. And the people I've brought in are more than talented: They're honest, loyal, and caring. They become friends. I have good instincts in this respect.

At first, Elisabeth didn't want to have anything to do with the skating world. She worked for a company that specialized in marketing and entertainment, and I'd met her while I was skating at an exhibition in Frankfurt. As she got to know me, however, she started to think working full time with me would be an interesting challenge. I'm by nature optimistic and like to laugh. I was interested in staging my own TV shows, creating my own productions in Germany, where there was no history of skating tours. I was tired of just performing in the United States. The fact that Elisabeth came from outside the skating world appealed to me. She had a broad knowledge of all kinds of entertainment and business. We were both workaholics. So in 1990 Elisabeth left the music business to become my manager. I was her first and only client, and we've worked together ever since.

But it's not just work that binds us. I can call her with any problem. She's a single mom with one daughter, and when she comes to visit me in Berlin, sometimes we sit at my kitchen table, look at the stack of papers she's brought for me to sign, and say, "We don't want to do this now." Instead we have a cup of coffee and catch up with our lives. Or we go on a little shopping spree. The business will come later. We don't see each other in person often enough.

"How long is Jasmine going to stay?" she asked.

"I don't know. Her attitude at first was to just spend one night and then move on to stay with friends," I said. "She implied she was just talking to me to appease you and her mother. I think I can convince her to stay another couple of days. She wants to watch me train this morning with Frau Müller, and then I'm going to take her to my gym. I need to start getting into touring shape if I'm going to skate this fall."

"Where do you get your energy?" Elisabeth said in wonder.

I groaned. "It gets harder every year."

I wasn't exaggerating. Last winter I'd told her I wanted to skate another one or two years. To do that, I had to prepare, and it takes me the same amount of time to prepare for four or five shows as it does for sixty. I'm not talking about an hour a day. It takes me six months of real effort to get into touring shape, four or five hours a day, and when I'm putting in that sort of time, plus the hours spent doing regular office duties—phone calls, paperwork, meetings, contracts—my life is put on hold. Which is why it's hard to make these decisions about whether or not to continue my skating career. At some point I need to get a normal life.

At the same time, what is a normal life? Define that. Everyone defines it on her own terms, and for me, skating is the life I've chosen. I'm so lucky to enjoy what I do. A lot of people must work at something they don't much like for a living, and they count the hours until they can stop and go home. Maybe they've never found what they're looking for. I'm one of the fortunate ones. I live to work. The time just flies by. I meet people mostly through work. It's what I love, and when you think about it, about one-third of your adult life is spent working. How sad not to love what you do. I have a plaque in my kitchen that reads: Life is not a dress rehearsal.

I must love it, because life on the road is anything but glamorous once you look behind the stage. The dressing rooms are not very nice. The buildings are cold. You travel all night, usually by bus. You have trouble getting regular sleep. The ice in the arena is too thin, too soft, too hard. But still the show goes on and you must skate. All these obstacles you have to deal with, but I'm adaptable. I'm pretty good at immersing myself in the world I'm in and making the best of it, even if things aren't the way I like them. I learned that growing up in East Germany, where there were many situations I'd have liked to change but couldn't. If we end up staying in a bad hotel while on tour, I know it's only for one night. I may not like it, but I'm not going to bitch about it. It doesn't help to whine. Because at the end of the day, the spotlight comes on, and you go on the ice—this is what you do. This is your life. It allows me to do what I love: perform for an audience. I've never lost my passion for that.

Frau Müller recognized that about me early on—that I needed an audience—and she used that knowledge to her advantage. For example, practice was generally boring for me, but as a teenager I used to train at the same facility as the speed skaters from the GDR. The boys would stretch and warm up in a second-floor gym that had a view overlooking the ice. Frau Müller knew their training schedule, so she always made sure we practiced when the speed skaters were in the gym. I always trained harder when they were watching me. My coach did whatever it took.

It was nearing the time I had to leave to meet Frau Müller at the rink, so I rapped on Jasmine's door. "Good morning." I waited, hearing nothing. "Hello! You awake?" My heart started to race with the fear she'd already left. Then I heard the rustling of covers and a muffled greeting inviting me in. I pushed open the door, and she was rubbing the sleep from her eyes. I noticed her backpack was unpacked. So she'd be staying. "Sleep well?" I asked.

"Like I'd been clubbed," Jasmine said. Even with her eyes puffy with sleep, she was a beautiful girl. She stretched her arms over her head, arched her back, and yawned like a cat.

"You still want to join me for my practice? You can sleep in, if you'd prefer."

"Do I have time for a shower?" she asked.

"A quick one. What would you like for breakfast? I have bread, fruit, and cereal."

"Just coffee, thanks. I'm not a breakfast person."

I frowned, debating whether to lecture her on nutrition so early in the day. She hadn't eaten much dinner the night before, either, pushing it all over her plate. "I'll grab you a banana in case you get hungry later. Ten minutes, okay? One doesn't leave Frau Müller waiting."

The rink where I train is called Hohenschoenhausen, a big sports complex. It's in what used to be East Berlin, about a half-hour drive from my apartment, depending on traffic. I have a parking place behind my apartment building, and as we climbed into my Mercedes, I tossed Jasmine the banana I'd brought for her. "Don't starve yourself, sweetie," I said, trying to sound casual. "You can't be an athlete without eating properly, and coffee on an empty stomach doesn't count."

She nodded, tucking the banana in her purse, but unconsciously making a sour face. "Of course I remember very well what it's like to be starving yourself to be thin," I said. "Figure skating can be very cruel that way, yes?"

"Yes."

"I always had problems staying thin, especially in the summer."

"You never would have known it from your pictures," she said.

"But those pictures were never taken in the summer," I said, laughing. "My competition weight was 112 pounds, but I'd go up to 120 pounds every summer. When I went on tour after the World Championships, I'd put on weight very quickly because I was eating American food that I never ate at home. I loved muffins and ice cream. I loved the supermarkets. I'd go in thinking I was going to buy apples or bananas and would come out with bags of junk food. All the healthy foods were there, but I wasn't disciplined enough to select them. America is a fast-food country, with big portions. Supersized portions. I always felt that since the country was so big, the food was big, as well. And I'd get big just being there. It was so difficult to keep my triples over the summer because I couldn't get my body in the air. I'd pick French fries off the guys' plates at 11 o'clock at night, or eat buffalo wings at midnight. That's the worst thing you can do. You can't go to bed hungry, but you learn, eventually, to eat raw vegetables or fruit after a show. But I love food! Sometimes you have to let go. But I let go too much, and after four weeks on tour I was, like, whoa, what's going on with my body?"

Jasmine laughed as I puffed out my cheeks and stomach. The traffic was light, and it promised to be a beautiful spring day in Berlin. I drove through Alexanderplatz, the old square dominated by an immense 600-foot television tower that has a café at the top that affords a breathtaking view of the city. The TV asparagus, it's nicknamed, a huge stalk overlooking Berlin. "It was a daily fight," I said. "A daily fight. But when the time came, and I really needed to, I could always get the weight off."

"What was your secret?"

"Starving. Extra training. Spending extra time on the bike."

"If I put on eight pounds in the summer, I'd never get it off," Jasmine said.

"It's easier not to put it on in the first place," I agreed. "But you can't starve yourself all the time. The truth is you can eat anything you want, as long as it's in moderation. You can have a piece of chocolate if you feel like it. It just shouldn't be the whole bar. Your body craves for things, and if you give it what it wants in little pieces, it's fine."

"My boyfriend likes to say that the only way to get rid of a temptation is to give in to it," she said.

"There's some truth in that," I agreed. "You just have to learn not to go overboard. I don't count calories. But when I was young it was very, very difficult for me. Weight was a topic of conflict for many years."

"Between you and your coach?"

"Yes. And between my parents and my coach," I said. "The only time my parents really got involved in my skating was to express concern over how I was eating. They were interested in my skating, of course, but my mother wasn't like the skating mothers you see today, overseeing every little thing. She left that to Frau Müller. But the one time my father stepped in was after he learned I wasn't getting any real food at the ice rink. I was training seven hours a day, but I was only getting water and rice at lunch, with a few slices of apple and artificial sweetening. Disgusting. That was my lunch, because she wanted me to lose weight. It made him so mad he went to the ice rink and told Frau Müller this had gone far enough. 'I'm taking my daughter out of training school,' he told her. 'She's starving. She's suffering. It's wrong!'"

Jasmine laughed at my imitation of my father. "How old were you then?"

"Maybe seventeen. But it was interesting, because I learned something about myself. I'd already decided I wanted to become a champion, a great athlete, and I trusted Frau Müller. She could have told me anything, and I'd have done it. So even though I knew my father would support me, and that rice with apples for lunch was not enough when you were training, I decided I'd better keep all my complaints about my coach away from home. I left my problems at the rink. Because I knew it was really my fault. Why would I always put on weight? It wasn't necessary. So after that, whenever my parents asked, I always said everything was fine. Training was going well. I was eating well. Then once a month they'd meet with Frau Müller at the ice rink, and she'd complain about all the problems I was giving her, how I didn't train enough, I was too lazy, I'd put on too much weight. They'd be in shock, because really I was not very big. My body was changing, my metabolism was changing, which every girl goes through, and there was nothing I could do about it. And my coach was telling me I was too fat. She didn't like it that I started to get a woman's body. She thought I should have a more girlish body. Frau Müller did not like seeing my more womanly form emerge, and the truth is I was never comfortable in my body for many years."

"Because you had boobs?"

"It helps to be thin in figure skating. You know that. You can rotate faster in the air, you're lighter, you can jump higher, and in a subjectively judged sport like ours, let's face it, appearance matters. Looks matter. That will help a beautiful girl like you, Jasmine. It wasn't like I had big, heavy . . . well, you know. But they were there, and they needed to be supported, and we couldn't find the right materials to work in those days. Plus, there are certain tricks to constructing a costume that we hadn't yet learned. The worst was when I came out of my costume during an exhibition number in Paris in 1987."

"You're kidding."

"I'd wanted to wear a costume that looked like a bustier, but it took months to be made, and when it finally arrived I didn't have time to try it out in practice. The first time I skated with it was during the Paris exhibition. Big mistake. The top of the costume was made of elastic, and in the middle of a spin I could feel it sliding down, down, down."

"The costume?"

"Yes. The bustier with the very stretchy straps. It was stretching. Suddenly I felt a draft. When I finished the spin I had to pull the top back up, and the rest of the program I skated with my arms pressed up against my sides. I was afraid to move my arms. I knew one of my boobs had popped out of my costume, but I didn't think anyone had a picture of it."

"Oh, no."

"Yes. Whoever took the picture didn't do anything with it for three months, until February, just before the Calgary Olympics. Then they published it. It's still out there on the Internet, and it's just terrible. The Canadian coach made a big deal out of it, saying I was trying to win the judges by wearing sexy costumes, which was pretty stupid because I was so embarrassed by the incident."

"What did Frau Müller have to say?"

"Actually, she laughed. She said it was proof that I'd have been better off with a girl's figure instead of a woman's. It wasn't until I met the Canadian choreographer Sandra Bezic that I became comfortable with my body. That was in 1989 when I was doing a production with Brian Boitano called *Canvas on Ice*, filmed on a glacier in Alaska, and in Paris and East Germany. I was always wearing sexy costumes and saying, 'Oh my God, my boobs are in the way.' And Sandra would laugh and say, 'You should be happy and proud that you look like a woman out there.' I don't have these problems anymore, thank God, because Jef Billings, who's designed my gorgeous costumes the last few years, knows exactly how to create outfits for me. And his seamstress, Emily Assayag, is a genius at constructing them."

Jasmine was staring out the window as we drove along the tree-lined boulevard. "I don't think a coach should ever make you feel uncomfortable about your body," she said.

"But it was only when I'd gained weight," I said. "It wasn't like it is today, when parents say: 'No, no. I don't think what you're doing is right.' And the coach tiptoes around, afraid to be too strict or the parents will go to somebody else to coach their child. Frau Müller was the most successful coach in the entire world when I had her, so we had to accept her the way she was. Democracy is great, but sometimes a coach has to be a dictator. Sometimes there's only one way. For a skater, eating normal portions is too much, and I ate pretty normally. That's when Frau Müller was strict. She even took me to her house for the weekend sometimes, where she would eat exactly the same portions that I ate. We'd diet together. So she was fair. Then she'd put me on skis and would send me into the forest. So I was active while eating very little, which is the best way to lose extra weight."

"Starving you, then sending you into the forest on skis. She sounds like a character out of the brothers Grimm."

I began to wonder if Jasmine had a strong enough mentality to be an athlete. "She was my teacher, and as such always had to be ready to crack the whip. I never saw her soft moments, because she wouldn't show them to me. It wasn't because she didn't have them. I never saw her cry. She was always strong and independent, and I trusted her. Listen, Jasmine, to be a world-class athlete, most of the time you need to go beyond your pain limit. You can get to it on your own, but you need someone to push you over. Otherwise you'll never improve. And for that you need a coach. It's very difficult to be a great coach and at the same time to be a friend. That's why I never called her by her first name: Jutta. It was always Frau Müller, and still is.

"Your coach can't be the enemy. She must be someone you trust, because, after all, you're on the same side. You're pulling on the same rope. But neither should your coach be someone you go have a drink with, because then it gets easy to say: 'I don't want to do this today. We'll do it tomorrow.' The coach's goal is every day to get the best out of you, to suck the greatness out of you, and that's hard. Frau Müller had to be my enemy sometimes. I had to hate her. I had to feel aggressive toward her, so I'd be able to work under her discipline. If she'd been my friend, I'd have walked off when she told me to keep doing a triple, even if I fell fifty times. There has to be an element of fear. That's the only way, I think. That's why some other skaters quit. They couldn't take her anger and turn it into their own energy, as I learned to do. They'd just get more frustrated and think they were worthless. I was very strong, very stubborn, and could forget very quickly. I could walk off the ice after she'd screamed at me for half an hour, and after a fifteen-minute break come back on, and we'd look at each other and say, 'Okay, now we work on something else.' Then you start from scratch. That's something you should be able to do. I was always pretty good at sleeping problems away. Every day's a new day. That's important for a skater, or any athlete. And you know what? She would hug me as well, and say, 'Kati, I just want your best.' And I always believed her."

Jasmine was thinking about what I'd said. She kept looking out the window, and as she did so took the banana out of her purse and peeled the top and took a bite. Perhaps it was a tiny concession to me, or perhaps all the talk about food was making her hungry. Whichever, I was happy to see her eat.

"Every day I had to step on the scale at the ice rink," I continued. "Every single day. I always ate two meals at home, breakfast and dinner, and she'd tell my parents to just cook me a small steak in the morning. At night, if she was trying to get me to lose weight, they weren't supposed to feed me anything at all. It was crazy, really. So at 6 A.M. I'd have a small steak and a piece of bread, then rice and some pieces of apple for lunch, and at night, instead of eating a proper dinner, I'd sneak chocolate that I bought from the store."

"I could live on chocolate," Jasmine said.

"Me, too. In figure skating there are two types of girls: the ones who are always careful and eat healthily, and the ones who like sweets. I liked sweets. I loved sweets. And having something forbidden just makes it sweeter, you know? The pocketed fruits are always more toothsome than the rest. So, in secret, I'd eat chocolate instead of dinner, and I'd think I was starving myself, but in fact I was putting on weight. It's something you have to learn. Starving yourself just makes you gain weight faster, because you end up eating sweets between meals."

"Or you make yourself throw up. I've known some girls to do that."

I frowned. "That's very scary, but I can see how it happens, the way the fashion industry is. The way the models in the magazines look. No wonder kids today are all screwed up. Then you go into a clothes store, and nothing fits. It's frustrating. You think the ideal woman has to look like those skinny girls, but it's not healthy."

"Or they have orange juice and laxatives for dinner. Nice."

"It's so stupid, because now there's so many healthier foods than when I was your age. In the GDR you couldn't just buy the vegetables and fruits you wanted at the grocery store. In December, you could buy oranges and apples, but not strawberries. In August, you couldn't get oranges, but you could buy strawberries. Rarely could you find bananas. Now you can buy any fruit or vegetable you want, anytime. Which is great, except a lot of them have been genetically modified and don't taste like anything at all. Big huge red apples with no taste."

"Better to eat chocolate.

I laughed. "In moderation, of course."

"Everything in moderation."

"Ah, here we are," I said, pulling into the parking lot. "The world-famous Hohenschoenhausen. My rink."

I grabbed my bag and led Jasmine through the skater's entrance, pausing to say hello to the security guard. A class of young skaters was on the ice, dressed in leggings and gloves and short skirts. I changed into my sweats in the dressing room, and for the next twenty minutes I stretched. The Zamboni machine was just taking the ice when I began to put on my skates. "When I competed I always had the same routine," I told Jasmine. "I had to tie my skates three times, right one first, left one next. Then I'd untie them again. Right, left, right, left. For luck. I couldn't sit still. I kept moving and moving the entire time. And you? You have a superstition?"

"I had my lucky Band-Aid last season," she said, smiling. "It started out to cover a blister, but then the blister went away and the Band-Aid stayed. I mean, I changed it. I just always wore it."

"I guess in some ways everyone's superstitious," I said. "Some people keep the same teddy bears with them they had as a child. Or you're not allowed to pass the salt directly to someone. You have to put it down on the table. Or you eat the same breakfast. I had three little stuffed animals that my physical therapist had to hold in a certain order before a big competition: a little angel, a fluffy animal, and a little thing that wasn't anything at all. A little mascot. The angel always had to lose both its wings every season. One of the wings had to come off at the European Championships, and the other wing had to come off at the Worlds. Believe me, in an Olympic year we had a dilemma: three competitions and only two wings. Then every year I sent the angel to be repaired so the wings would be ready to fall off the next year. It was tricky, because my therapist wasn't allowed to pull the wings off. They had to fall off by themselves, with a little encouragement. She had to be rough on the angel, to loosen the wings, but not too rough."

"That's an elaborate superstition."

"Yes, but it worked. And of course before a really big competition I'd pray to God. That was the only time. I was like: 'Please, please, please, if You exist, make me win. I will go to church then, I promise.' And afterward I'd forget about it until the next big competition, and then I'd pray, 'I'm sorry I forgot about You, but if you're really up there, and you help me, I'll come to church, I promise.'" Jasmine was smiling and shaking her head. "Twice a year I'd pray. It's not very fair, but I didn't want to leave any stone unturned."

"Whatever works."

"Exactly. Okay, the best place to watch the practice is from the bench. If you get cold just come back here to the dressing room. I'm on for an hour. I'll introduce you to Frau Müller beforehand."

"Have fun."

That made me smile. I liked to talk to other skaters and have a good time on the ice when Frau Müller wasn't around, but it was always serious work when I took the ice with my lifelong mentor and coach. I enjoyed it, yes, but I only invited her to help me a couple of times a year, usually for a week, and in that one week I got more done than if I trained alone for four weeks.

Some coaches just teach to make a living. Other coaches, like Frau Müller, live for the sport. She skated in the 1950s, but she was never a star herself. In those years the GDR never did well internationally. At one point they hired an English coach, Megan Taylor, to try to improve their performances at the World Championships, but she left after one season. "Those East German skaters have what it takes to go to the World Championships, all right," the Englishwoman told a reporter after she'd left. "But only as ticket takers."

Frau Müller never forgot that slight, and it motivated her in her career as a coach. She proved the Englishwoman wrong, too. Under her tutelage, GDR skaters won ten World Championships between 1969 and 1980. Her daughter, Gabriele Seyfert, and Anett Pötzsch and Jan Hoffmann all won twice, and I won four times. Frau Müller was the most successful coach of her generation.

To work with me she drove down from Chemnitz, where she still lives, and stayed the week with her daughter, who lives in Berlin. She's seventy-six now, and still very fit. Once we got on the ice and I'd introduced her to Jasmine and dispensed with the pleasantries, it was the same as it always was. It's not like Frau Müller cracked the whip, like in the old days. But we still worked hard. "What do you want to work on today?" she asked. Our relationship has changed over time, which is nice for both of us. It's woman to woman. She listens to me if I say I don't want to do something. At the same time, she makes me run through my routines more often and more intensively than when I'm alone.

When I haven't been on the ice for a long time, the truth is I get scared about doing the jumps. It sounds silly, but it happens, and just having her there helps. She tells me it's crazy, that I've been doing the double axels and double loops since I was twelve. She helps me technically if I'm having trouble with a particular jump. But no more triples. I'm done with triples now. My very last triple toe loop I kissed good-bye at the Goodwill Games in Lake Placid in 2000.

When I was competing, we used to go through everything in every practice. We'd divide my program into three parts and would repeat all three parts three times. We set priorities for each session and tried to vary it so it wasn't boring. I was always someone who liked to move. I was restless, and I wanted to jump and leap around, which was why I always hated compulsory figures. But inevitably you get to a part in the practice where you have to keep repeating something over and over and over again to get it right. Then it's boring, but this is how you learn, regardless of age. That's why I've always tried to pick music that I liked, because I knew I'd have to listen to it a few hundred times.

I liked it that Jasmine was there watching my practice. Even now, the worst thing for me is when nobody's there, or when people are there but aren't paying attention, when they turn their back and are talking to somebody else. I hate that. Some people, like Brian Boitano, love to practice and do it only for themselves. He'd get onto the ice and would go into his own private zone. I needed the Olympic or championship environment, getting to a competition and having other skaters sharing the ice, having the judges watching. I needed some kind of pressure or attention before I got better, and I'd skate better every day once I arrived at a competition. I remember one practice in Cincinnati during the 1987 World Championships. The American Caryn Kadavy was skating her Spanish free program, and we were sharing the ice with five or six other skaters. When I heard Caryn's music, I loved it and started improvising to it as she was doing her program. Four thousand people were in the stands watching, and I totally drew everyone's attention away from Caryn. She was furious with me, I learned later, jumping on her bed and hitting her pillow she was so mad. But I didn't do it on purpose. I just loved performing. I didn't do it to take attention away from anyone else.

The way you practice is the secret to success. As an athlete it's your most important tool. It's the foundation of your whole mental approach: If you know you've practiced well, you'll be confident in the competition. If you haven't practiced well, you can't expect to do well. That's why it was always easier for me if there was someone on the ice who pushed me. Someone I could compare myself to. It was difficult for me in Chemnitz after I became world champion, because then I had no one training with me who skated at a world-class level. What kept me going was my natural competitiveness. I didn't want to lose. I don't know where it comes from, but even now this competitiveness comes out. I fight for things. I don't give up on things. And I suppose it helps that I'm stubborn, because I don't like to give up on something until I succeed.

Because of this I think I could have been good at many different sports. Soccer. Tennis. I'd have loved to play tennis, because your opponent is right there, and you can fight against her, which is kind of nice. The problem with figure skating is you never really have an opponent in front of you. I probably would have behaved like John McEnroe, always putting on a show to be the center of attention, getting mad on the court, making jokes. In figure skating I was never able to totally let my emotions out. I had to repress them. If I missed a jump, I couldn't show it. I had to keep skating, keep smiling, pretending nothing had happened, which is difficult for me. Even during the 1988 Calgary Olympics, when I was skating to *Carmen,* I was frustrated at not being able to show my joy at skating well and landing all my jumps. It would have been completely out of character, because I had to do a double axel at the end of the program, just before Carmen got killed. I landed it, and in the next moment I was getting a knife in my stomach. As I lay dying, I couldn't show how happy I was.

Eighty percent of the desire to become champion must come from inside the athlete. The rest, however, must come from the coach. A runner, left to his own devices, will run as comfortably as possible. But somebody has to be there to tell him: "No, no, no. If you want to be the best, you must push yourself past your limit. Otherwise you'll never improve." This is the thing that makes you get better and better and better. Frau Müller impressed that on me at an early age. When I was tired, she was there to push me to the very limit. She sometimes would yell at me. She was the only person I ever allowed to do that. No one else. A few people have tried, but I don't allow it. I understood why she was doing it and never took it personally. So when we came off the ice, everything was fine.

At the same time, Frau Müller was good at patting me on the back and telling me when I did a great job. But she made sure she wasn't patting me on the back all the time. When we traveled, she always made sure we walked around town and saw the sights. She was wonderful that way. She'd darn my mittens if they had holes in them. And she always sent me the sweetest cards on my birthday and at Christmas. She still does.

So I know she had a soft side. I know she cared about me as a person, not just as an athlete. But she believed, and I agree, that discipline is a big part of life. Frau Müller knew that you couldn't be both a great coach and a friend.

5
Speaking Openly

"You're *completely different around her,*" Jasmine said.

"Am I? In what way?"

"You can tell how much you respect her. It's just a very cool thing to see. And you work hard!"

After the session we'd driven back to my apartment, where I was preparing salad with turkey for our lunch. Jasmine was setting the table. She'd been unusually quiet, which I hadn't known how to interpret. Now I realized she'd taken in a lot. "When I was younger," I said, thinking back, "it used to upset me when people said all I had to do was step on the ice and the judges would give me the marks to win. I didn't train six hours a day to have people tell me I won because I was beautiful. Of course, I don't mind now," I added, laughing. "It helped, I'm sure, a little bit. But I like to think I won because my programs and triple jumps were a little better than the others, not my looks. And that took a lot of work."

I set our salads on the place mats on the kitchen table, and we sat opposite each other. "You two are all business," Jasmine said.

"That's because we don't want to waste each other's time. We've developed a really nice relationship. A coach has to change through the years, too. If they take you when you're young, they have to accept that when you grow up, you'll have your own mind, your own set of experiences to draw from. At first that was hard for Frau Müller, because when I was a girl I'd have done anything she told me to do, and I trusted her. But when I became an adult I *also* learned to listen to my body. A skater, or any athlete, has to listen to her body first, and trust it. It took some time, but Frau Müller learned to let me be a partner, not just a student. That's why, after all these years, we still work together so well."

After the session, Jasmine and Frau Müller had talked a little while about Jasmine's skating, because Frau Müller had seen her compete at the German Nationals. My longtime coach could be charming when she wanted to be, and she'd been charming with Jasmine.

"You are lovely on the ice, my dear. You charm the judges in a manner that reminds me of someone else," she'd said, smiling in my direction, "and that you cannot teach. You must learn to cultivate it."

Jasmine had beamed. "Thank you, Frau Müller."

"Work hard and set your goals high. Katarina always wanted to be the best, and this is what you must also aspire to. Never be satisfied."

"I won't."

"I'll watch your progress with great interest."

Frau Müller couldn't join us for lunch, because she wanted to meet her granddaughter downtown to go shopping. Still, it was wonderful that they'd met, and Jasmine came away thrilled with her words of praise. She was also amazed that a woman her age still had such spark and vitality.

"I'd love to have her energy when I'm her age," I said.

"What are you training for, if you don't mind me asking?" Jasmine asked me. "Are you still entering professional competitions?"

"My competition days are behind me," I said, laughing. "But I have several television shows in the fall, in Germany and in America."

"Nice.

"You know who I love to watch in those shows? Kristi Yamaguchi. What's she like?"

"She is so sweet. Just the nicest person. She's like my American sister. I've adopted her. She has a family of her own now."

"I'm curious: How competitive are you with each other on tour? I mean, do you razz each other about who gets the loudest applause?"

I laughed. "You never want to be upstaged, but the important thing is for everyone to do well so the audience enjoys the show. Some nights you feel better than others, so as performers you're able to feed off each other. Any teasing is entirely good-natured. Four months of touring is hard enough without having to keep a popularity scorecard. But I'll tell you, Jasmine, it's a great experience for a skater, the perfect vehicle to display your talent. For skaters who love to perform, who aren't afraid to work, who want to put themselves in the most capable hands, to perform in the best costumes with the most interesting choreography, Stars on Ice sets the standard. It's the best show to be in."

"But four months. Wow. Long time."

"Since 1989 that's how I've been spending almost every winter. The last two seasons were the first time in fifteen years I didn't tour at all, and I didn't really miss it."

"Why not?"

"The bad thing about touring, even though it sounds glamorous, is you leave home in October to rehearse and come back in April. Your life is on hold. And of course the generations are changing, which makes it even more difficult. Kristi wasn't on my last Stars on Ice tour. She was starting her family, and believe me, I missed her. Neither was Katia, who had another baby at home. There was a cast of younger skaters. John Zimmerman and Kyoko Ina. David Pelletier and Jamie Sale and Anton Sikharulidze and Elena Berezhnaya, who were in the middle of the Salt Lake City Olympics pairs-judging scandal."

"That was nasty. What was your take on that?"

"It was a tragedy for skating. I was there, doing commentary for television, and though the Russian pair skated well, with a couple of small mistakes, it was clear to me the Canadians had won. There was absolutely no doubt. They really were transcendent. There are only a few times when a skating performance moves an audience, really moves you so you know what you're watching is art, and this was one of those times. Every element they did was perfect. It took my breath away, and I'd seen them do that program several times before. But not like that. And to do it in the Olympics! As a skater, to watch that and then see the judges put another pair first . . . well, I knew something was wrong. Some funny business. It was very sad for our sport."

"And having them both on the same tour? Was that awkward?"

"No, not at all. The Canadians never blamed the Russians, and the Russians never blamed the Canadians. They were both victims, really. So they were friendly. All of us were friendly. It was fun to be around the younger skaters, because they gave the show a new spirit and energy. They looked up to me and felt they could learn from some of my experiences, without making me feel old. So that was nice. But it's difficult to be away for four or five months. I missed my parents and my friends from Berlin. I missed the skaters I used to tour with. They become like your family, and over the years you develop incredibly close bonds."

I didn't want to get into it with Jasmine, but the truth was I found it difficult to really have open conversations with the other skaters the way I could with my old friends in the skating world. It wasn't the same. Friends you've known for fifteen or twenty years—you can get in an argument and a fight, then you sleep on it, and who cares? You move on. But if it's someone you've only known a short time, you must tiptoe around a subject. And I hate tiptoeing around. I'm someone who says what she thinks. I'm not diplomatic. I'm honest. But after I say what I feel, it's over, and I can move on.

During my last Stars on Ice tour, the Iraq war was just beginning. It was so difficult for me to talk about it, I felt like it was a dangerous subject to even bring up. That was a strange situation for me, who came from East Germany, a country where you weren't allowed to express your real opinions, except behind closed doors. And even then you had to be careful. Whereas Americans grew up believing they could express their opinions honestly and openly, whatever they were. Suddenly I was in a situation where I was a European, feeling more liberal than my American friends on the tour, reading papers and magazines from Germany, which of course were against the Iraq war. The information in them was entirely different from what we were seeing on CNN and other American television stations. The German magazines were painting a different overall picture. So I'd come on the bus and say, "Look, this is what I just read. You're not getting the entire picture of what's going on in Iraq." I thought they'd want to know what the rest of the world was thinking. But some of them didn't want to know. All of a sudden I felt I was back in the past in East Germany, where everything was dictated and judged and censored, and the newspapers only gave out what the government wanted.

It reminded me of something that happened in 1988 before the Berlin Wall came down, when Brian Boitano and I started to become friends. We'd both won gold medals in Calgary, and we were doing some specials together. He'd say negative things about East Germany, how people there weren't free, and even though I knew some of what he was saying was true, that my country had some things wrong with it, I'd defend it. "How can you say these things?" I'd ask him. "I do live in a free country. There are no poor people living on the street. Everyone has work. Everyone has food and a roof over their head." And Brian would say, "But you aren't free to speak out. You aren't free to travel." For me, the other things were more important. So I'd defend my country even though I knew in some ways he was right.

That's what was probably happening with the other skaters on tour when the subject of the Iraq war came up. They knew that in some ways I was right, but they defended their country anyway. I'll never forget the night we all watched the Oscars together. Michael Moore received the Oscar for best documentary film, and he was the only recipient who used the opportunity to say anything at all about the war. I supported his speech so much. "Finally," I said, "somebody used this huge stage to express his opinion on a subject of such importance." A few skaters looked at me like they wanted to strangle me. It was the strangest experience. With good friends, you can have different opinions and move on. You accept it. But I learned in America, the land of free speech, you had to be careful when you talk politics.

Jasmine pushed her plate away a little, leaving some of the small portion of turkey salad I'd given her. "What's it like living in America?"

"I love America," I said. "I do. I love their mentality: 'Let's just do it. Let's just try it.' That's something that's not very common for us Germans. Germans are always a little hesitant when they hear something new. In America, they're always a little quicker to listen to new ideas and try to make them happen. I enjoy their uncontrolled enthusiasm about something or someone they love. They're much more supportive of someone they see has talent. There's less jealousy. You can be successful, and people are honestly pleased for you. 'All right! She deserves it! She trained harder. She earned it.' In Europe and in Germany, we struggle with this, you know? We're like: 'What did she do to be so successful?' They're suspicious of it. It's interesting."

"I wonder why."

"I don't know. They're always looking for ways to cut you down to size. Like in Germany I'm always introduced as an ex-Olympic champion. You're very much an 'EX.' It's done, it's yesterday, okay? Former. Well, of course it's former, but being an

Olympic champion is something that stays with you forever. In the States, I'm always introduced as the two-time Olympic champion. Once an Olympic champion, you're an Olympic champion forever. Here, what was done yesterday, stays yesterday."

"I'd like to see California. Maybe just to travel. Not to train."

"So you should go! When you're young, that's the right time to go abroad and expose yourself to completely different points of view about countries and traditions and the world. It helps open your mind. It's so different than if someone only lives in her own little town or village. Once you travel you learn you can't always judge things so harshly. You have to accept different things, different traditions and cultures, and respect them."

"My English is pretty terrible."

"That's the second time you've mentioned that. I hope that's not the real reason you're reluctant to train in America."

"I'm just saying. It makes me self-conscious."

"Learn by doing. That's the best way. You'll learn English once you get there. I took some lessons in school, but it wasn't enough. I'd be afraid to speak, because you think people are laughing at what you're saying. But they want to help. I had a friend, an American ice dancer, Judy Blumberg, who was always great. She was always: 'Speak, speak, speak! That's the only way to learn.' And when I made a mistake, she'd explain it to me. Once I bought a gift for someone, and Judy asked: 'What have you got there?' And I said, so pleased, 'Oh, I became a present.' She laughed and said, 'Really? Someone put a red ribbon around you and now you are a present? How nice.' Only then did I understand the grammar of it."

"My grammar's so bad it's not funny," Jasmine said. "I understand English okay, if someone's speaking it to me or I'm watching a movie. But when I speak, who knows what I'm actually saying."

"You'd can't worry about making mistakes or you'll never learn. Once Brian Boitano and I were doing an interview to promote an ice show after the Calgary Olympics. What I wanted to say to the interviewer was: 'I keep trying to express myself.' What I actually said was: 'I keep trying to impress myself.' All Brian did was smile to himself. He didn't correct me during the interview, because he thought it was funny. Only later did he explain it to me."

Jasmine poked at her salad and smiled. "Bernard doesn't like the idea of me going to the States, since he thinks most Germans are already overly influenced by American culture. All the movies and TV shows that come from Hollywood. What's that all about? He thinks we should be more Eurocentric."

"Ah-ha."

"What's that mean: 'Ah-ha'?"

"Now we're getting to the crux of it."

"Of what?"

"It just seems there's more to it than what you were telling me about your reluctance to train in America. Bernard disapproves, no?"

"He just doesn't see why a German coach can't teach me just as well. A young Frau Müller. He's proud to be German."

"We're talking about becoming a champion skater. It isn't enough to be proud of your country. You have to go where you'll learn the most."

"That's the part he doesn't really get."

"Let me ask you this: How supportive is he of your skating? Did he come to watch you compete at the Nationals?"

"No, but Bernard was working. He watched it on television. He wouldn't let the customers at the bar change to the football."

"That's nice."

"He thinks it's pretty cool that I'm, like, fourth in the country."

"Does he understand how hard you'll have to work to become first?"

She laughed. "No! He already thinks I'm way too self-centered about my skating. I mean, 'Get over yourself, girl. Get a life.'"

"What does that tell you?"

"That he's a guy. He'd like me to think of him as the center of the universe. That's what they all want, isn't it?"

"Not all. But quite a few. Some men just don't believe a woman's career should take precedence over them. Is he one of those?"

"I don't know. It's not like we sit around and talk about it. But he's pretty traditional. His mom doesn't work."

"Do you love him? You haven't said."

She looked down at the floor, a little embarrassed. "We don't use those words exactly, but it could get to that, I think. We just haven't known each other that long. But I want to."

"Want to be loved?"

"Well, yeah. I hate the singles scene, just hooking up. I feel, you know, special around him."

I smiled, not unsympathetically.

"He wants us to move in together."

"Really?"

"Well, not right away. But he's always thinking ahead. Planning stuff."

I was thinking: "Jasmine, at your age you shouldn't let a boy decide your future, especially one who doesn't encourage you to pursue your dreams. At sixteen you should try new things." At the same time I couldn't help smiling because I remembered how I felt when I first fell in love. You may only be young once, but you never forget it.

"I fell in love for the first time when I was eighteen," I said. "Two years older than you. His name was Ingo. He was a drummer in a rock band. So I know where you're coming from. Have you ever read a book called *Captain Corinna?*"

She shook her head.

"It was my favorite book as a teenager. A teacher gave it to me. Corinna was an athlete, a volleyball player, the captain of the team. She's seventeen, and she meets a guy. She likes him. She starts going out with him, riding on the back of his motorcycle, taking time away from her sport for him. She starts drinking and begins to lose her conditioning. But she's happy. She really likes the guy and doesn't know what to do, because she doesn't want to lose him. I read the book and felt I was going through the exact same thing. I still have it, and if you like, I'll give it to you."

"What happens?" she asked suspiciously.

"Oh, at the end she pulls herself out. Goes back to practice, and once again finds her passion for volleyball. It doesn't work out with the guy. I felt so close to the character of Corinna. It was one of the few books about competitive sports for girls. At the time I didn't talk to my parents about this stuff. Just my girlfriends."

"I know that routine. So what happened with Ingo?" She asked it reluctantly, like she knew this was going to be a cautionary tale.

"He was twenty-five—seven years older than me. He had to go into the army."

"No way."

"Way. When I first started going out with him, Frau Müller was very suspicious. He started taking me dancing at the clubs, and I was staying out late at night. She was afraid my relationship would take away from my focus on skating."

"Well, duh," she said.

It made me laugh. "The thing is, as an athlete you live in a different world. What's pretty normal for other teenagers—going to discos, drinking, smoking, hanging out with your friends and still doing well in school—is poison for an athlete."

"So Frau Müller got Ingo drafted into the army?"

"No, of course not. In the GDR all the young men had to serve in the army, but someone from my sports club, one of the officials, made sure Ingo was stationed as far away from me as possible." I laughed at the memory, which after all these years was funny. But it wasn't funny at the time. "I was in the south of the GDR, and they sent Ingo to train at a base that was the farthest to the north. When he had a twenty-four-hour leave, he couldn't make it down to see me. The train connections took too long. So that was pretty much the end of our relationship. That's a true story. I read it in my Stasi files."

"The secret police? Jesus."

"There was always emotional turbulence over Ingo. I was totally in love with him. Then the summer before he went in the army, when I was already an Olympic champion, he went back to his old girlfriend. I was heartbroken. We'd had a wonderful time together, but he didn't see it going anywhere. So I was totally heartbroken, crying, moping on the ice, that moment thinking that sport can't be everything in life."

"That's what I tell my mother. Sport can't be everything."

"Sport isn't everything," I agreed. "But neither is a boy. And there are certain times when sport has to be everything. Anyway, I felt I had to make a decision whether to fight for Ingo or forget about him and focus again on my skating. Which is when a funny thing happened. I went out to dinner with Ingo's stepmother, who was a younger woman, closer to my age. I had a good relationship with her. She invited me because she knew I was so sad that Ingo wanted to break up with me. I'd seen him that day with his old girlfriend, and I thought that Ingo's stepmother could help. So we went to dinner. I had a 10 P.M. curfew, and after we ate she brought me back to the hotel. We were on time, but I was too upset and wouldn't leave the car and go inside. I was crying and hugging her, because I thought my life was over. You know this feeling? I was totally crushed. She would take me in her arms and comfort me, and before long it was ten minutes past my curfew. I finally pulled myself together and walked into the hotel, and Frau Müller was there with her arms crossed. 'Come into my room,' she snapped at me. I followed her into her room, my cheeks still streaked with tears, and she began screaming at me. 'What a scene in front of the hotel,' she yelled. 'You're kissing and hugging and carrying on with that man, and it's past curfew, and probably all the other athletes are looking out the windows and watching you! Are you crazy?'

"I just looked at her blankly. 'What do I care about any of that?' I asked her. 'My life is ruined. And anyway, that was a woman.'

"'Oh! That was a woman!' she said. 'No, that wasn't a woman. You were hugging the whole time!'

"I couldn't believe it. I just looked at her and started laughing uncontrollably. 'Frau Müller, that was a woman!'

"'Now you're trying to tell me you're a lesbian!'

"Then I totally broke down crying and said, 'I am in love, and my heart's been broken, and that woman was a friend who was trying to comfort me.' I left her room and slammed the door I was so angry, and went to my room to cry myself to sleep. What a scene."

Jasmine was shaking her head in amazement, as I laughed at the memory.

"Over the next few days I realized that continuing like this wouldn't be possible. A guy can't rule your life and make you sad and break your heart. So what I did next was get back on the ice, get back in shape, and just go back to what I always wanted to do. I found my own path back. No one else could help me. I realized that things weren't going to work out with Ingo, and there was really nothing I could do about it. It was out of my hands. When you have a person in your life that you love, you have no control over what will happen. That was the lesson I learned. Skating, however, was something I could control. When I was skating, my destiny was in my own hands."

Jasmine was staring hard at me, biting her lip.

"Over the next two weeks," I continued, "I was totally crushed. My heart was broken, but I realized I wanted to keep skating. I didn't want to quit because I felt there was still so much to do and to learn. I was still Olympic champion. So this is how I guided myself back through the heartbreak, because I already had something I loved: my passion for skating. That's a wonderful thing to find in life, to learn what your passion is. This heartbreak with Ingo actually increased my love of skating. And I never let a boy threaten that again. It wasn't the last time I had my heart broken, but after that I always knew what to choose. My skating came first."

She was listening, but it didn't look like she believed me. "It can't be all about you all the time," Jasmine said. "I don't think so."

"In my life it is all about me," I said, laughing. "And at this point in your life, it has to be all about you as well, if you want to reach your potential."

"But any relationship has compromises. There's give-and-take."

"I always had relationships on the side, but my focus was skating. I loved flirting, to be with men, to have a special man, but I knew skating was my absolute priority. And that basically always stayed the same. And I was always clear about that with my boyfriends."

"Speaking of boyfriends, didn't you date McGyver once? The actor?"

"Richard Dean Anderson. Yes. Richard and I had a serious, intense relationship. It's way more complicated than I'm going to get into, but there were a myriad of reasons why it didn't work out. Part of it was culture shock. I was inexperienced, everything was new to me, the wall had just come down, there was a language barrier between us, he was famous, we were living on different continents, and the tabloids were constantly following us around. He wouldn't give up anything careerwise. And I wouldn't give up anything. And that only works for a short while. If you want to become really serious, to have the relationship work, then somebody has to play second violin. I haven't been willing to do that. A lot of times when things didn't work out with one of my boyfriends, it wasn't that we didn't understand or love one another. It was that each of us was too passionate about our careers."

"It sounds pretty self-centered."

"If you want to be the best at something, as self-centered as it sounds, this is how it has to be. Everything around you has to support you if you want to be the best in tennis or golf or skating or anything. You can't look left and right. You have to have the blinders on. If you want to be the best at something, everything else comes second and third. If you want to make compromises, sport is the wrong business to be in. I can't think of any exceptions to this. If you want to be Olympic champion, nothing can be allowed to stand in your way. Look, Jasmine, you can make compromises. You can make time for your boy. You can have a good time. But you should know any compromises you make take away from your chances of success. Sport is definitely a field that you cannot make compromises in. It has to be more than a 100-percent commitment. One hundred percent is not enough. If it's not more than 100 percent, you won't make it. Everything else has to be selected out. That's a decision you have to make. You can't have it all."

Her lips were pursed in a stubborn pout. "I guess maybe I'm not like you," Jasmine said.

"Of course you're not. Everyone's different. You have to find out who you are."

"I don't know if I could live like this."

"Like what?" I said, arching my eyebrows.

"Like you live. Single. Calling other skaters on tour your family. No offense, but maybe someday I want to get married. Maybe someday I'll want to have kids and a family. If you do that it can't be all about you."

I stood up and took my plate to the sink. Then I turned and faced her, controlling the anger in my voice. "As a teenager everything seems so much bigger than it really is. Jasmine, you are so innocent, just as I was when I was your age. You think your love is so big, and it is in a way, because it's your first love and you don't know better. You're not willing to make compromises because you don't know there are other choices."

I stopped myself, but I was thinking that in twenty years she might look back on all the loves that had come and gone in her life that were more significant than that first one, on all the heartbreaks that were bigger and more painful. But I knew she had to learn that for herself. I wasn't going to tell her that the boy she was seeing was probably wrong for her. That she was too young. That he was too old. That the whole thing would probably be over in a year or two, whether she went to America or not. She'd have to find that out for herself. She'd have to have her own heart broken. She'd have to go through her own pain. That was part of growing up.

"I know that what I feel is real," she said.

"You have to live your own life, Jasmine. That's how you become the person you're going to be twenty years from now. Adults can't shelter their children from all this stuff. You have to see for yourself. You have to make your own mistakes."

"Who says I'm making a mistake? You've never even met him."

"I'm not talking about your boyfriend. I mean in life. You have to make your own mistakes in life. That's how we learn. You have to discover whether or not you're serious about your skating."

"I'm serious. I just don't see why I have to choose between skating and my boyfriend."

"When you're young, and you make a decision, you think that decision will last a lifetime. You think that you'll have no other chance to change. But life isn't like that. You can change paths at any time. No decision is forever. You're constantly making decisions that three years later you'll want to change. So you can go to America, and if it doesn't work out for you as a skater, you come home. You go to university. You can always go back to school, Jasmine. And if the boy's the right boy for you, he'll be there. If not, you'll find another love. Or you'll find him again later when the time is right for both of you. Sweetie, you may not want to live the way I live, but you'll never have the opportunity to reach your potential if you put a boy ahead of your talent now. Your talent has to come first. How would you feel in ten years if you didn't pursue your skating? Wouldn't you regret what might have been? It's your choice."

She was silent.

"You don't have to make that choice today."

"I know that," she said sullenly.

"All right then. I've got to make some phone calls."

"I didn't mean to make you mad."

"I'm not mad. I want you to speak openly with me, the same as I promise to speak openly to you. All right? That's the only way any of this will do any good."

She looked away, out the window. "Can I ask you something?"

"Of course."

"Do you ever wonder if you've given up too much for your success? If it was too great a sacrifice to become a great skater?"

I thought for a long time before answering. "I used to think about that. When I was your age I used to see other kids playing when I was going to the rink to train. They could go to the disco, go crazy at parties, eat whatever they wanted, whenever they wanted. Yes, it takes sacrifice to train six, seven hours a day. To show so much discipline. But at the same time, I've gotten so much more back. So now, when I sit back and wonder if I'd rather have raised a family or have my life the way it is, I think: 'No, I'd rather have my life the way it is.' But that's not a conclusion everyone would come to. You should never compare your life to anyone else's. Maybe someone with a family thinks: 'God, this is the best you can have, a husband and children.' But she shouldn't judge my life, anymore than I should judge hers. You don't make decisions for others. You make them for yourself."

"I wish you'd tell that to my mother."

"Well. She's your mother. She's used to making decisions for you."

"No lie."

"I only have to make decisions for me. I've thought about changing that, about getting married and having a family. I've seen marriage work. I see it in my parents, whom I love dearly. I admire them for being together, for loving and respecting each other and making each other happy. But that doesn't mean I'm troubled about not having that for myself. I've been proposed to, but I said no because I knew it would be a lie to say yes, because I knew it wouldn't last forever. Sometimes you meet someone and you feel it's the right person but the wrong time. I believe in destiny. If it's meant to be, maybe years later you'll meet the same person again and now you'll both be on the same page of your life. You never know. There's so many possibilities out there, you always have to keep your mind open. Nothing is impossible."

"Have you ever dated someone from the skating world? Another skater or a coach? Someone whose life is more on the same schedule as yours?"

"Mostly I've dated people outside the skating world."

"Is that because the men are mostly gay?"

I gave her a look of mild shock and started laughing. She had fallen prey to the old cliché.

"You said I could speak openly," she said.

"There's not as many gays as straight guys in figure skating," I said. "That's a misconception. The pool for a girl is bigger than you think. Still, I'd rather have someone from outside the skating world in my personal life. I want to be with someone who's successful and independent, exactly the same as me, except in a different field than skating. But that makes it difficult, of course, if no one is willing to give up anything." I shrugged my shoulders and smiled. "I've had wonderful relationships along the way. I was together with someone for seven years. A part-lifetime companion, I call him, because there really hasn't really been a word invented for that kind of relationship. Passionate long-distance affairs. Short-term sexual interests. Mad, crazy, unconventional loves that fizzle with time and distance. Call it what you want. My relationships just haven't worked out permanently, maybe because of my traveling so much, being so committed to my career. I haven't been ready to give that up for someone. I'm not complaining. I don't fit into a traditional mold. And you know what? Maybe no one had enough strength to love me."

Jasmine was silent, thinking. She'd been listening, but I was pretty sure half of what I was saying was going right over her head. Maybe more than half. But, who knows? Maybe in twenty years she'd look back on this conversation over the kitchen table and it would suddenly make sense. "Anyway," I said, "enough about that. At three o'clock I'll come get you and we can go to the gym to work out. Sound good?"

"Sure."

"Then maybe later we can go through some of my scrap-books. If you're interested."

"Sure. I'd love to."

I squeezed her shoulder and smiled. Sixteen was a tough age. "Later, then," I said, turning to go up the stairs to my private office. It occurred to me suddenly that Jasmine had just been politely pushing her salad all over her plate and had never finished her lunch. It made me wonder, not for the first time, if the reason things had never worked out for me with the guys was that I was a terrible cook!

6

Thoughts on Relationships and Marriage

O_{ur} *conversation lingered in my head,* and I wasn't able to work. I wasn't used to talking so frankly about my personal life, and doing so made me feel like I was part of a cheesy, hopelessly romantic movie that the audience watches with tears streaming down their cheeks, thinking: "Yes, this is what life should be about. Love!"

Relationships, marriage, having children—of course I've thought about them. I grew up in a very happy family. However, I've long since accepted that the way I work and live makes it difficult to build a relationship like the one my parents have, that long-distance relationships work for a while but don't last. For a number of years I lived almost half the year in America, either Los Angeles or New York, and the other half in Germany, so it was almost like living two lives at the same time. I had my apartment in Berlin, my friends in Berlin, my family there, and then I'd go to America to work and to tour. The two parts of my life never meshed. So if I got into a serious relationship, there was never enough time together you could share, moments that afterward you could look back on and remember together. What I needed was someone who traveled with me the whole time, who shared my entire life, but that's not what I wanted in a man. I didn't want someone whose life revolved around mine.

So that's been my dilemma. I always knew I'd rely on myself to make a living, that I'd never depend on somebody else. I grew up in a country where a man was not expected to take care of a woman. Men didn't make a whole lot more money than women in the GDR, so it was always taken for granted that I'd work. And that didn't change for me once the Berlin Wall came down. If anything, that life-changing event made me feel I had to prove I was better as a businessperson just to be accepted as equal to someone from the West. I had to be better because I didn't have a network to tap into. I couldn't make any mistakes. I had to work harder to get where I am now. It's still a man's world.

My career has been my priority. As a woman, though, in some ways that makes it more difficult when it comes to relationships, because it's hard to keep from trying to control your destiny in all facets of your life. If I'm dating somebody and he tells me he doesn't love me anymore, there's nothing I can do about it. I have to accept it. It's not like skating, where if you lose a competition you can try to be better the next year. There are some things that are not in your hands. Needing to be in control discourages you from taking risks in your personal life. Maybe along the way there was a path I could have taken, but I was afraid. Maybe there was a time when I met somebody and could have said: "Okay, I'm going to let go with this man. I'm going to give up my need to be in control, because I want to have a family." But I never did, because I was afraid. I was afraid something would happen, that the man would stop loving me and the marriage would fail, and I'd have given up my other life for nothing. I'd have sacrificed my career. So I turned back.

Anyway, it's all changing. Today, it's not unusual for a woman to have a career. A lot of women live like I do without feeling bad or guilty about it. It's common. People now accept that my lifestyle is the result of me choosing a different path rather than having misguided priorities.

I've never fit into any traditional structure. I've never thought things were forever. When you get married you have to say, "Till death do us part." So far I haven't been able to promise something like this. I know through my experience that things aren't forever with me. Eternities come and go. The men I've been with were always perfect for the particular stage in life I was living through at the time. I loved them, but I always knew somehow it wouldn't last forever. I was able to enjoy the moment without thinking too much about the future. What's tomorrow? What's in ten years? I was never able to picture that.

People say that when you meet that special someone, you immediately know he's the right person. You just know it. I believe that. And it's happened to me. It just never lasted a lifetime. The institution of marriage was never a life goal for me. But I haven't ruled it out, I'm not against it. My life is constantly changing, I travel so much, going from project to project. It's hard to find someone who might become part of all that. It's easy to find someone who fits in with part of it, but not all. And if you don't grow together, if you don't share experiences together, you move apart. But I've learned to accept that. I'm fine. I've never thought, "Oh my God, I'm thirty-nine years old, I'd better get married." Never. I'm not panicked.

I've always liked the spotlight, liked the attention of being in the public eye, of feeling the satisfaction of doing a good job and seeing the reactions of people to my performance. But I know the most fulfilling feelings are to love and to be loved. It's as simple as that. That's what's most important. And life is best when you're doing the thing that you love, and you're also with someone you love.

What I want in a man is a real challenge, someone who makes me feel that I've met my match. The challenge is part of the attraction. I want somebody I have a lot of respect for. It doesn't matter how much I love a person if I lose respect for him. And respect comes from many things: how the man treats you, how he behaves, how he acts. How a man is.

Men are conflicted when it comes to women these days. I've seen it. A man dates you, and he knows how strong you are, but he doesn't understand there are also moments when you're just a woman who is helpless about certain things, who needs affection and attention and support. Some men can't handle that. They get confused when a strong woman behaves just the opposite. I like a man if he understands your weaknesses as well. I've always been able to show my vulnerable side when I'm comfortable with a man. I don't show it in public. But if something goes wrong, and I'm home, I'm not afraid to cry my eyes out.

Here's a small example of how men are conflicted these days. A few years ago I boarded an airplane in Los Angeles, and I was lifting my suitcase onto the overhead rack. Nobody helped me, and they could see it was frickin' heavy. The men in first class were just sitting there watching, and the people behind were all waiting. I finally got it up there, but afterward I actually had the guts to say, "You know what? In Europe somebody would have stood up and helped me with the suitcase." I said it in a nice way, though, with a smile.

I sat down, and the man behind me leaned forward and said: "You know, we're confused here in America. Because once you offer to help a woman, she's apt to say, 'No, no, no, I'll do it myself.' They want to be so independent that we don't know when to let them be independent and when to behave like a gentleman."

I had a really nice conversation with him about it, because it's confusing to me, too. I'm an independent woman who supports herself, so I definitely want people to think of me as someone who's self-reliant and confident. Someone who makes her own decisions. But at the same time I want to have a guy open the car door for me. I like it when men wait for me to pass through a door first and when they help me with my luggage. In that context, I'm an old-fashioned woman. And my dad has always been such a gentleman. I have to fight with him if I want to carry my own suitcase, even the kind with rollers. He just won't let me. So it's generational, too.

Maybe it's something we understand better in Europe, because European women were independent a little earlier than women in the States. Now we've returned to appreciating traditional mores. A woman can be independent without always flaunting it. You can fight so hard for your independence that you lose your femininity. And that's what this stranger in the airplane was trying to point out to me, that American women have tried so hard to eliminate gender as an issue that men don't know how to handle themselves anymore. The women want to prove they can do everything alone, so okay, you go, girl, lift your luggage up. European men are much more comfortable with behaving in a gentlemanly manner toward women, and as I grow older I realize how nice it is to be treated in this conventional way.

My experience has been that American men are different from European men in other ways, too. It's more difficult to have men as friends—just friends—in America. At least it has been for me. In Europe, if a man takes you out for dinner, it doesn't mean anything. But in the United States if a guy takes you out for dinner, it's a date. As a woman, you have to make sure they know it isn't. Then if you go out a second or third time with them, they expect something in return. This was new to me. Naively, I'd be thinking: "Oh, I've made a new friend." And the man was thinking I was interested in him romantically.

Maybe it's because of the way I was raised, or because I have so many business dinners, but when I meet somebody I always think he might become a friend. Now I realize that in the States most men think that if it doesn't go somewhere, it's not worth the time and effort. Maybe it's different when you're younger, but when I was living in Los Angeles in my early thirties, all I was looking for was some sex. (Just kidding!) But seriously, I wasn't looking for a romantic relationship. I wanted company. But you had to make that really clear. That was weird for me, completely different from the way things worked in Berlin.

So I'm learning. Slowly but surely. When I look back at my old relationships, I remember them as good times, happy times that were right for that period of my life. I don't feel bitterness about any of them. Not now. At the time, of course, when I went through the pain of having my heart broken and couldn't function for days because I was paralyzed with sorrow, I'd be bitter. Getting your heart broken is always bad. The first time is the worst—it's like that for everyone—but there's never a good time. So you swear you'll never date again. You promise yourself. And it could be five minutes later some guy walks by who makes you forget about your promise, and, ever hopeful, you start down that road again.

Even some experiences with jerks can help you make better decisions in the future. It's all part of the puzzle that's your life. It makes you into the person you are and can change you for the wiser. I've had relationships with challenging men before, but I was too young for them to last. I couldn't speak English well enough to communicate when there started to be a problem. That was sometimes the source of difficulties, because I missed the finesse of speaking in my own language. I'd tiptoe around the things that were difficult to express. The exact words I needed to say would elude me. I'd have been better off with a dictionary beside me at all times, because when there was a problem in a relationship with an American, I'd want to point it out and talk about it, but I just couldn't. I was blocked by the subtlety of the language. I wasn't able to convey exactly what I felt, or I'd say it too clumsily. Or maybe I was just too young and stubborn to make the necessary compromises. So when things didn't work out, it was probably for the best. But those are only things you realize with time.

As you mature you begin to understand it's not so much about the things you want in a man and in a relationship, as the things you don't want. When you're young, you might sit down with a piece of paper and write: "This is what I want in Mr. Right, and this, and this. My perfect man. I want, I want, I want." But you don't really know, and you're not going to find him the way you've imagined him in any event.

Later on, after you have more experience in life, maybe your expectations change. You're ready to make more compromises. But you're also definitely not ready to accept certain things you simply can't live with. You know what they are. You won't deal with them anymore, no matter how perfect a guy is in other ways. You know what you can't accept.

So you learn from experience. That's what's important. I'm not perfect. Relationships are still a riddle to me. But one thing I've learned: Even the wrong decisions make you wiser.

7

Fitness, Playboy, and Me

*W*hen *I was in the third grade,* I transferred from my regular school to the sports academy in Chemnitz for prospective Olympic athletes. As I mentioned earlier, the focus there was on sports first, then academics, and it was the training place for the most talented young figure skaters and speed skaters from Chemnitz, an industrial city of 300,000 people. It was a sophisticated system used throughout East Germany and was one of the reasons our small country was so successful in the Olympics.

On a typical Monday I had five hours of academic classes, plus two sessions of compulsory figures, two sessions of free skating, and then an athletic workout, away from the ice, that lasted sixty to ninety minutes. We'd play soccer and volleyball, or we'd go running or swimming, or cross country skiing in the winter. We had training camps for two weeks at the Baltic Sea in the summer, and I loved those camps away from home. It was always hard training, but it was fun. We played tennis, did weight lifting, jumping, sprints, conditioning—everything you can imagine. My favorite was when we played soccer, indoors, in a medium-sized gym rather than on a big soccer field. The gym had four little goals in it, and four players played at a time, each with a goal to defend. The rules were you had to kick the ball into one of the goals, it didn't matter which one, as long as it wasn't your own. You could bounce the ball off the walls to pass it to yourself. I was good, and one of my strategies was to miss the ball and kick the others in the shins on purpose. Then I'd take the ball away from the poor girl and put it in the goal. I was a competitor, it didn't matter what sport.

Every other day I had an hour of ballet, too. It was a real science, this regimen, and I'm certain it gave us an advantage over the American skaters twenty years ago, who didn't do all the off-ice training we did.

I explained all this to Jasmine on the way to my fitness center, because off-ice training is something I've continued to do all my life. All those different sports I played when I was young helped my body become flexible, fast, and strong. If you only do one kind of sport, especially a sport such as skating, which uses such specific muscles and repetitive motions, you ignore the fitness of the rest of your body. It's the whole package that's important if you want to reach your potential and stay free of injuries.

"I work out off ice every day," I told her. "I'm probably one of the few professional skaters who does that. Six days a week, actually, and one day off for your body to rest. I always had back problems until I started traveling with my physical therapist. So now I joke that when I was young, I traveled with my coach.

Later on, I traveled with my boyfriend. Now I travel with my physical therapist."

"How long do you work out?" Jasmine asked.

"Two hours a day, but it's not necessarily two consecutive hours. Maybe I start with forty-five minutes on a bike. Then I'll take a break and later do some weights. Then later, stretching. You can't do the same thing every day. You have to vary it. If you do jumps, you don't do them every day, but every two or three days. If you work on one muscle group with weights one day, you leave them out the next day, so they have a chance to recover. And you should stretch. Any stretching exercise is good. Flexibility is really important."

"I don't have time to work out for two hours a day," Jasmine said. "Between school and my skating, I barely have time to eat."

"That was the advantage of going to a sports school. Once we started competing in October, all we did was concentrate on our sport. I trained and skated—no academics. Today in Germany a girl who goes to a regular school gets on the ice at three o'clock, and the coach can only ask her to do three hours of work. Three hours a day isn't enough to create a world-class athlete. I used to spend three hours a day just for compulsory figures. Can you imagine? I hated compulsories because they were so boring, skating in circles and circles and circles."

"I thank God every day they got rid of them," Jasmine said.

"It's totally changed the sport," I said. "But to be honest, as much as I disliked compulsories, in some ways they were good. You had to pay your dues. You had to patiently work your way up the skating ladder, and that gave you time to get mentally stronger. Each season we had very specific goals. We had time to learn to handle the pressure. And without compulsories, look what's happened. The champions started getting younger and younger, which meant they turned pro when they were too young. Like Oksana Baiul, who won the Olympics in 1994 when she was sixteen, then turned pro and fell off the deep end for a few years—drinking and partying and nearly ruining her life. She's okay now, thank God, but that's too early to have that kind of success, and all the money and freedom that comes with being a professional. To have everyone telling you how wonderful you are. Having seen her skate, having admired her beautiful ballet movements and amazing artistic talent on the ice, I had wanted to watch her grow into one of the greatest figure skaters of all time. And it's sad for me to think of how she cut her amateur career so short. It kept her from developing into a legend. And there was Tara Lipinski, who won the Olympics in 1998 when she was fifteen and immediately turned professional. I saw her on the Stars on Ice tour in 2002, when she was just nineteen, and saw how much pain she was in. She finally had to have a hip operation, and to have a hip operation at that age is ridiculous."

"I don't see what that has to do with compulsories."

"Since they aren't spending hours and hours on compulsories, young skaters have time to work on the difficult jumps. They have to in order to master them. Maybe their technique isn't perfect, but they can land the triples because their bodies haven't matured, and they are still so small and quick. Over and over and over again they practice them, and each time they land, it generates three times their body weight on the landing foot. That's the physics of it. I wonder sometimes if my body would have broken down by now if I'd followed their regimen. I doubt I'd have had my longevity. It's too much. Your body is still developing, and over and over again you do these very difficult jumps that generate massive amounts of stress. I never had a serious injury that kept me out of a big competition. Now everyone has injuries—to their feet or their knees or their backs. I see that Evgeny Plushenko, the Russian world champion, twenty-two years old, has constant pain in his knees from all his quadruple jumps. I don't think it's right. But when you're young, you don't think very far ahead. You just think in terms of the next day, the next week, the next competition. You don't think about injuries that could threaten your long-term health. The sport has gone too far, I'm afraid. It's breaking down too many of the best young skaters. Or maybe the skaters aren't doing enough off the ice to protect themselves."

"Protect themselves how? By refusing to follow their coach's orders?"

"We did so much working out off the ice—not just in the winter but all year long—that our bodies were prepared to survive the impact of landing the jumps."

"But you had time for all that off-ice training."

"Yes. So you make the time. A lot of skaters, all I see them do is skate. That's not enough, Jasmine. When you're young, sixteen or seventeen, you take your body for granted. You think nothing will ever happen to you. I see a lot of young skaters who just put on their skates and get on the ice without ever warming up. It's crazy. You have to warm up. And even if you're fit, every day you have to work out. It doesn't matter what sport you play. Golfers and tennis players, even Formula One drivers, have learned this about their sports. You have to make the time. It doesn't matter if it's before your practice or after practice. That's how I've been able too keep myself healthy through the years. The more fit you are, the fewer injuries. Find a partner to train with. That really helps. It's very difficult to do it alone. So you find a companion, even one who plays a different sport. Or you go to a fitness studio. Find a friend, make an appointment, because once you make a commitment like that, it's not so easy to say, 'Oh, I'm tired today. I think I'll stay home.' You'll always find some excuse."

"How about the 'There's only twenty-four hours in a day' excuse. That old chestnut?"

Jasmine could be pretty funny. "Try to develop a routine if you can," I said, laughing. "Then you can adapt your schedule to it. What about setting aside time the first thing in the morning? It's easier to work out in the morning, because late in the day most people are exhausted. Get up a little earlier than usual and go for a run. Then go to bed a little earlier on the other end."

"I hate running. I thought running was bad for figure skaters."

"Not at all. I've been running since I was a little kid. Ever since, it's been part of my regular workouts. Just be sure to vary your routine. Do a short, fast run one day to build up your aerobic conditioning, then a long and slow one the next day to make you feel good. I call that the feel-good workout. Long and slow. And if you want to really build your heart rate, do interval training: fast, slow, fast, slow. Run a minute, walk a minute. Or if you want to improve your stamina, run as fast as you can for two miles, for example. Time yourself. Or run as fast as you can for five minutes, then rest five minutes. It depends on what your goals are. It's important to train your whole body, not just certain sets of muscles. Exercise opposite muscles. Stomach exercises should be balanced by workouts for your back. Work the bicep, then the triceps. Always exercise in balance. Push, then pull. Up, then down. Left, then right. Twist, then turn. One good exercise which is very simple is to lie face down on a mat, lift your arms out to either side, then move from the waist up, left and right, slowly. Constant movement. It's great for your back. Pilates is great. Biking. Power walking. Swimming. Rollerblading. Any movement. And variety is key. If you bike for an hour, stretch out afterward for a long time, otherwise your quadriceps will get shorter and shorter. Once that happens, you get back problems. Your body is one big chain reaction waiting to happen. It's all connected. Conditioning it is a science."

"Do you know any exercises that will help me with my double axel?"

"All of these will, because they'll make you faster, stronger, and more flexible. But you can also buy special boots called Jumpsoles. It's an American product. They look like platform shoes with weights on them, and you put them on and jump up and down to build up those muscles. They were invented for basketball players. I've used them the last few years, and it's amazing. They're really heavy, and you step in only with your toes, so your heel is off the floor. This builds up your calf muscles and thighs. If you do jumping exercises with the Jumpsoles for a few weeks, I promise that you'll find you can jump higher in skates. But only keep them on for twenty minutes at a time, no more, because they're really awkward. It totally works."

We'd arrived at the building where my health studio was located, a modern facility on Friedrichstrasse called Six One Physioconcept. I'd discovered it when I was rehabilitating my back

following an injury, and now I relied on it for preventive maintenance. They had all the new exercise machines, plus some excellent physical therapists. After working out I could get a really
good deep-muscle massage, which is something I have after
every show when I'm touring. That's one way I've prevented a lot
of injuries. If your muscles have been working hard, they have to
get relaxed. And that's what a deep-muscle massage does.

I introduced Jasmine to my friend who works there, Clint, an
American dancer who pays the bills by being a trainer for the
new gyrotonic machine in the studio. It was specifically designed to strengthen the back, which is a problem area for many
skaters, myself included. The ice is hard as concrete when you
land after a jump, and rotating two or three times in the air
causes a lot of torque in your upper body. Put it together, and
you have the ideal recipe for developing a bad back. This particular machine works on a pulley system and offers circular resistance, so you twist and arch against an even, stable force. The
range of exercises you can do with the gyrotonic machine is
amazing, based on yoga, swimming, dance, and gymnastics. I
started my usual circuit, exercising all the major muscle groups
in under an hour. Unless someone is looking for bulk, it's better
to do many repetitions against steady resistance rather than a
few repetitions involving something really heavy. You build up
endurance and burn off more calories that way.

Jasmine worked out at three stations under Clint's guidance
and finished about ten minutes before me. She watched as I
went through my last two stations. "You're strong," she ob-
served, testing the station I'd just left.

"You should have seen her pumping iron before her *Playboy*
shoot," Clint said with a chuckle.

"So it's true?" Jasmine asked. "My boyfriend told me he'd seen you in *Playboy*. I wasn't sure whether to believe him or not."

"Believe him," I said, smiling. "A big seller all over the world. It sold out in Germany within hours."

"Why'd you do it? I mean, I could never have some stranger taking pictures of me without my clothes on that you know will wind up all over the Internet. You must have been paid a lot of money."

"It was an adventure, actually. I was surprised."

"Weren't you worried it would hurt your career?"

I shrugged. "A little. Not too much. I talked it over with Elisabeth, who was the only one who knew, and she thought it was a good idea. She could have talked me out of it if she'd wanted. I listen to her advice. *Playboy* had been asking me to pose for them for almost ten years, since 1988. I wasn't interested at that time because it didn't fit into my career. But when they asked again in 1998, I thought, 'Why not?' I had a successful professional career that was getting better and better, so it wasn't like I was taking off my clothes to jump back into the public eye. I did it to be a little rebellious, I suppose. I'd been the ice princess, the little girls' idol. I thought, 'The heck with it, let's do something more controversial.' Elisabeth and I decided it together."

"Did it just come out in Germany?"

"Oh, no. It was worldwide. The offer came from the Chicago office of *Playboy*. They were very professional, and they convinced me it would come out the way I wanted. I was allowed to choose the photographer, and the time, and the setting. If I didn't like the pictures after they were taken, I could call it off. I had the final say."

"So where did you decide to shoot it?"

"Hawaii. It was a big secret. I was there with Stars on Ice as part of the tour, but I didn't tell any of the other skaters. I told them I was staying there for another three or four days for vacation. Nobody knew. It was important to me the pictures be beautiful, and Hawaii is such a beautiful place. I didn't want it to be done in an erotic way where you lie in bed and look into the camera like: 'Here I am. Take me.' The whole idea was for it to show a woman celebrating her own body, comfortable with her femininity. Pure. Not lustful. And it worked. It was so tastefully done. I think I was the first athlete to be photographed in *Playboy*, which opened the door for others. It was fun, actually. One Canadian writer had to write a story about it, and he went out, found a copy of *Playboy*, and brought it home in a brown paper bag. His wife saw him with it and asked: 'So how are the pictures?' And he answered, 'Oh my God, she's got the greatest calf muscles!' I was laughing so hard when I read it. It was very funny."

"What did your parents think? Mine would have freaked."

"That's another funny story. It came out in the Christmas issue, and I hadn't told them. Elisabeth had agreed to do it for me, actually, but she kept putting it off, and of course she never did. So I had to do it. I sat them down, very nervous, and said: 'I have something to tell you.' My father interrupted me: 'Oh, no. You probably did something crazy like pose naked in *Playboy*.' My jaw dropped. Huh? This is the way it always is with parents. You always hear that you shouldn't underestimate them, and it's true. They know what's going on without letting on that they know. And my parents are great in that they never interfere. They wait for me to ask them to get involved in things that concern me. They thought the pictures were fine, too. They didn't embarrass them. In Germany there are naked pictures everywhere, in the newspapers and magazines every day. So it's not as big a deal as it is in America. The main thing I wanted was to make sure the pictures only appeared in *Playboy* and wouldn't be published in any newspapers, and the cover wasn't a photo of me in the nude. Those would all be on the inside, so I wouldn't have to walk through airports looking at a magazine cover of myself in the buff. It was also important to me that it wasn't out there for the kids. I didn't want the pictorial to end my skating career. Even the big paycheck I received wasn't enough to make up for that. I still had to appeal to children and families as a skater. And I didn't lose any jobs because of it. In fact, the *Divas on Ice* television show was signed after it came out. I got a lot of compliments on it, even within the skating community. Once people saw it, they thought it was beautifully done."

"What about afterward? Did you have a lot of creeps bothering you?"

"No more than usual. But there were a lot of funny things that happened. Like I'd be walking through an airport, and I'd see someone with the issue of *Playboy* in their hands, and they'd see me, and their eyes would go right to my chest. Straight down—zap. Lots of guys would send pictures for me to sign, but I'd only sign the cover. They still do, in fact. But there's not one single signed picture out there of me naked. Instead, I'd send them back the pictures and include a signed skating photo. Women bought the magazine, too. Lots of them, which surprised *Playboy*. They'd buy a copy for their men, and have me sign the cover so they could put it under the Christmas tree."

"That's a riot," Jasmine said.

"It was actually a really exciting month. The attention it drew was almost like winning a third Olympic gold medal. I enjoyed it so much I kept asking myself why I hadn't done it earlier. It was so positive. I mean, you can't please everyone with the decisions you make, but you can try to maintain a level of class and professionalism, and I think that was done. I was at an age where I was comfortable in my own skin, and I just had fun with it. I wasn't embarrassed. Athletes in general are more comfortable with their bodies than most people, because their lives are all about their bodies. I was doing interviews about the magazine shoot, no problem. Anyone who was critical of it, I don't think they'd seen the photos. Being nude on the beach, or nude in a waterfall—it's natural. Nudity is perceived much more normally in Europe. Young women walk around topless in the Tiergarten. When I was a young girl in East Germany, the country was well known for its nude beaches, and I used to go to them until I was sixteen. Then I had to stop."

"What do you mean? Why?"

"No one made me stop. I just decided. I'd finished second at the World Championships, and I got recognized at the nude beach by a figure-skating fan. That's the first time I thought, 'Uh-oh, I shouldn't do this.' This guy had seen me skate on TV, and he came up and said, 'So nice to see you.' Only he wasn't looking at my eyes. That's when I thought, 'Uh-oh.'"

Jasmine laughed. "Well, you were probably the only figure skater with anything to look at. Most of us have nothing up there."

"I used to be so self-conscious about my body. I told you that. It wasn't until I met Sandra Bezic, Brian Boitano's choreographer, that I stopped worrying about it. She had a woman's figure, too, and was very beautiful and stylish. She'd wear cashmere sweaters, nice perfume, Louis Vuitton bags. She was elegant and classy, and she was the one who introduced me to all that. I learned from her that less is more. I look at my pictures from 1988, when I won my second gold medal in Calgary, and I was wearing so much makeup it wasn't funny. I admired her so much, both her work as a choreographer and as a person. She used less of everything. And she would tell me, 'Finally there's a woman in figure skating, so be comfortable with your body the way it is.'"

I laughed at the memory. Sandra was the one who had made me feel comfortable about my place in skating. She was more than just a beautiful and feminine woman: She was a choreographer of incredible talent. She walked into my life at the right time. It was at the end of my amateur career, and she was the choreographer of *Canvas on Ice*, the special I was filming with Brian Boitano. I realized what she'd done for Brian's career, how superb her work was, and she took me under her wing.

Working with her was totally new and exciting for me, because I'd never worked with somebody as an equal before. Until then I was always the student, the kid. That's how Frau Müller treated me, and that's how the choreographers who worked with Frau Müller treated me. Sandra very much saw me as an equal because I was a two-time Olympic champion. At the time I didn't know what that meant. But she did, and she made me appreciate it more. So few people have won two gold medals in figure skating, only Sonja Henie and me in the ladies singles, and I've become more and more proud of it as time has gone by.

Sandra brought *Canvas on Ice* to life, and after that I invited her to choreograph my television special of the opera *Carmen*—the character I skated in my long program in the 1988 Olympics. I got the producer, Thomas Buerger, to hire her, and without Sandra on the project I certainly wouldn't have been such a great Carmen. She talked me through things, woman to woman, as my friend. She tried to give me a mental picture of how to act things out. It was so different than when I was competing as an athlete. I felt more like an actress.

I'll always have a special feeling for *Carmen*, which was being produced by HBO. That's what I was doing when the Berlin Wall came down in November 1989. We were filming in Spain. It was a night scene, and Thomas Buerger came onto the set and announced: "The wall came down." We couldn't believe it. I especially couldn't believe it. "Yep," he said, "I just saw it on the news."

We kept filming all night long, and I finally drove back to the hotel in Seville around 5 A.M. and turned on the TV. I got goose bumps watching it. The wall came down! I kept running that thought through my mind. No one knew what would happen. I couldn't even imagine how my life would change, and I was both excited and nervous about it. But I couldn't worry about it too much right then. I was committed to doing the film. I wanted to fly home to see what was going on in Berlin, but I knew that I couldn't.

We ended up filming the last scene of *Carmen* in Berlin on Christmas Eve. It was very emotional on several levels. I was going to get killed in the scene—it was the same death I'd died in my Olympic long program—and Brian Boitano was in a big hurry to go home for Christmas. I was so angry with him.

Christmas comes every year, but this movie was once in a life-time. How could he be in such a hurry? So we shot it, I got killed, and he flew off in a plane. That was the end.

It all worked out, though. The two Brians, Boitano and Orser, got Emmys for *Carmen*. And so did I. For that, we could all thank Sandra.

8

Sarajevo Olympics, 1984

"*You look so young,*" Jasmine said.

We were upstairs in my office, my scrapbooks spread out on the floor around us. Jasmine was looking at one from 1984, the year I won my first Olympic gold medal in Sarajevo. I was eighteen.

"Were you nervous?" she asked.

I smiled. It seemed so long ago. I had to think hard to remember my feelings. "I came there expecting to win. That's what I'd been training for. I'd been second in the World Championships in 1982, and fourth in 1983. So I was at a stage in my career where I was prepared to win. But I don't remember being especially nervous."

"Tell me everything. Tell me about the Opening Ceremonies." Jasmine's eyes were shining with excitement. It was the first time during her visit that I'd really seen her animated, seen her face come alive. The Olympics can do that to any athlete.

"But I wasn't at the Opening Ceremonies," I said. "The women always skate the last weekend of the Olympics, and Frau Müller didn't want me to be there for two weeks before competing, because I'd miss all the practice time I usually had. Looking back, it's kind of sad to have missed out on all that, but it seemed perfectly normal at the time. The first Opening Ceremonies I ever saw was when I covered the Olympics for CBS in Albertville in 1992. The truth is that in 1984 I had no idea what the Olympics meant until I came back home and found bathtubs full of letters. People kept recognizing me on the street. Not just in Germany, but in America, too. It was only then that I knew the Olympics were the chance of a lifetime. It's like the whole world stops and watches for two weeks. Everyone talks about it the next day. Very few events are like that in the world."

As Jasmine turned the pages of the scrapbooks, looking at the newspaper and magazine clippings, reading the stories that had been written about me, I told her as much as I could remember about the Sarajevo Games—the first of my three Olympic experiences. We stayed in the Olympic Village, which was a complex of apartment buildings. It all seemed very strange, like I was going to training camp in a foreign country. It was exciting, too. We had a big team, which was nice for me, because when training I hardly ever crossed another athlete's path. I met some of them, and it was really a feeling of being on a team, because in the dorm our sports officials had placed a big board with all our results on it, and medals were drawn in to show who had won what. You felt: I want to be part of it. I need to help the team. I was really skating for my country, which in some ways was awkward but was very interesting. Figure skating is about as individual a sport as there is, but suddenly I had the feeling I was skating for all the other East German athletes there.

Sadly, I never went to see any of the other competitions. I didn't have time for it. I really wanted to concentrate only on my skating, so I made myself have tunnel vision. About the closest I came was watching the bobsled team prepare its sled. They were polishing their runners in the dorm, and I was polishing my little white skating boots in the same room. I remember us watching each other as we did so. But I didn't watch them going down the course.

It was terrible being the last event on the slate. I hated it. Everyone else was having fun and celebrating after their competitions were done, and I still had to wait, had to prepare, had to concentrate.

Oh, it wasn't all business. We went to the big marketplace in the center of Sarajevo and shopped for sweaters and pewter plates. I watched the men smoking their long wooden pipes. You'd see athletes from other countries in their team uniforms. Of course you'd always prefer others to your own, but, bummer, we were never allowed to trade.

The American Rosalynn Sumners was the reigning world champion, and later, of course, when we both skated for Stars on Ice, she became one of my closest friends. We'd talk and laugh about the times we competed against one another. I went to her wedding last year and watched her walk down the aisle, smiling radiantly, filled with happiness, and it made me cry with joy.

But we weren't friends then. To do my best, I had to develop a kind of aggressiveness before a competition, so I convinced myself this was not a friendly fight. It may have been a friendly environment, but the Olympic Games were still a competition, and Roz was the enemy. That's what I always tried to think. The opponent is your enemy. You live and you let die.

Now I look back and go: Ay-yi-yi. There are more important things in life. Wouldn't it have been nice to have been friends with Roz when we competed against each other? But I was young at the time and had a different view of the world, and my world was so much smaller. I'd only experienced competing in sports and going to school. That was the world in which I lived, so that's how the world went round for me. My opponents were my enemy, and I would fight them. And I honestly believe I had to think that way if I was going to succeed. To be competitive, a certain amount of anger has to be inside you. Healthy anger. You have to be able to go out there and say: I will kick your ass. That isn't true for everyone. Brian Boitano was more about trying to attain a standard he'd set for himself. He'd go onto the ice and would enter a zone of his own, and then he'd skate. Brian Orser wasn't his enemy when they staged "The Battle of the Brians" in 1988. In fact, they were best friends.

So, everybody's different. But I know that fighting attitude helped me before a competition. I was born that way. There's a certain amount of competitiveness that's naturally in you, ingrained, and that's often what separates a champion from just another world-class athlete. There are a lot of world-class athletes. But to be able to deliver at the moment that it counts takes an inner confidence and maybe even a kind of cruelty you need inside you. You must be utterly insensitive to the feelings of your opponent.

There are many words that have a negative connotation in life that have a positive meaning when it comes to sports. Words like "cruelty" and "insensitivity," which are necessary elements in becoming a champion. "Dissatisfied" is another: not being satisfied with the position you're in. "Greed": being greedy for success. All athletes need to be greedy. There's nothing wrong with being greedy in life, either: taking in as much as possible, as long as you can do so without hurting people. You have to strike a balance.

I had to have the thought: I'll show you! That's what gave me a competitive edge. You should be able to turn that hardness off when the competition is over, win or lose. Then you become just a normal human being again. But if I had been friends with my opponents, close friends, I couldn't really have competed well against them. I had to feel: This is my enemy. That's because as an athlete you have so much pride, and if you lose you're pissed. You're upset. And it's easier to be upset at somebody you don't like than someone who's your friend.

That's what makes sport so great: to share a passion with someone who shares the same passion. Even if it's your enemy, you're partners. It's like being partners in crime.

I always looked calm before I skated, but that was just on the outside. Inside, I was always a volcano. And the secret was—and I suppose I learned this for the first time in Sarajevo—I knew I was able to deliver under pressure. I knew that what I could do in practice, I could do in competition. I was very confident in this ability to deliver. That was my strength.

It's a funny thing, but there's almost an attitude of sloppiness about it. Some skaters get those thin lips and look so serious and scared before they skate. But for me I was—well, there's a German word for the way I was: Burschikos. It means "tomboyish." And for all the talk of me flirting with the judges—one sportswriter referred to me as "the belle of Karl Marx Stadt" in Sarajevo—that's the way it was for me on the ice. Tomboyish. I wanted to be aggressive in a somewhat insensitive way. A lack of sensitivity is what you need to compete well. I kept my head down, seeing no obstacles, like someone who could walk right through a wall. I never talked to anybody backstage. I'd stay in my own little world, warming up. All the time, just warming up. The Russian girls I competed against, Kira Ivanova and Anna Kondrashova, skated so strongly and beautifully in practice. But they were rarely able to deliver under pressure. And even Rosalynn Sumners wasn't consistent. In Sarajevo she made two big errors near the end of her long program, doubling one triple jump and singling a double axel. Even though she had one perfect 6.0 for artistic impression, those mistakes were enough for me to win.

At last I could celebrate, except now the Olympics were over and everyone had to leave. I remember returning home on the train with the whole team, and how people were waiting on the platforms at every station to greet us, because we'd done really, really well. It was a big celebration all over East Germany, and we met the president and had a few receptions. But because the World Championships in figure skating came soon afterward, I never really had a chance to celebrate. The World Championships were held in Ottawa that year, and it was there that journalists started to compare me to Brooke Shields, who was starring then in *Blue Lagoon*. All of a sudden I was a Brooke Shields look-alike, which made me more famous in the States, because everyone knew who she was.

Many years later I met Brooke in Sun Valley when I was there for a skating show. She came right up to me and said, 'Oh my God, it's like meeting my sister.' Everyone had told her we looked alike all those years, too.

One advantage of being from East Germany was that even after winning my first Olympic gold medal, I was still able to successfully manage my time. There were no endorsement deals to distract me. It was forbidden. I did get some benefits, which the sports officials called privileges. It was nothing like what I'd have gotten if I'd lived in America, but I was now able to get a car. It was a Russian-made Lada, and I still had to pay for it, but the benefit was I didn't have to wait for ten years, which is what a normal person from East Germany would have had to do. And I got a bonus of about $15,000. That's how I paid for the car.

If I'd been from the West, from a capitalist country, I almost certainly would have stopped competing after winning in 1984, because I could have made so much money from endorsements and speaking engagements and TV shows. I'm sure I'd have turned pro. Which is why, looking back, I'm glad I grew up in the GDR. It gave me some values I've kept with me. Regarding money, for instance. Okay, it's great, but it was never really the motivation behind anything I did. That's easy to say, now that I have it, but the truth is, I was never driven by the pursuit of money.

Far more important to me was to prove myself a great athlete. And to be a great athlete, you have to concentrate 100 percent on your sport and your training. Make that 110 percent.

9

The World Championships
in Cincinnati

Jasmine had reached the scrapbook of clippings from 1986, the
year I lost the World Championship to my American rival, Debi
Thomas, in Geneva, Switzerland. If it weren't for Debi, I would
have won five in a row. She was one of the athletes I most respected, a strong, athletic skater and determined competitor—
someone who could get her act together when it counted. She
was also an honest and straightforward person. She wasn't fake.
She showed what she felt, which was another thing I liked about
her. She was never one of the typical skaters who tried to smile
when they didn't feel like smiling. What you saw is what you got
with Debi, and I never considered her my enemy the way our rivalry was sometimes described in the press. There was no per-

sonal animosity between us. We weren't friendly because both of us intensely wanted to win.

"So what happened?" Jasmine asked. "How did you lose?"

"I fell in the short program," I said, remembering. "I rarely made a mistake in the short program, because that's when the pressure was greatest, when I felt the fists in my neck. It was usually my strength. But in Geneva, I fell on the loop in my combination jump. It put me in fourth place before the long program, so I was too far back to catch Debi without help. I skated well in the free program. My new *West Side Story* program earned me the first two 6.os I ever got in international competition. But, too bad for me, it wasn't enough. The short ended up costing me my title."

"Were you pretty upset?"

"At first. But I couldn't be too upset with myself for long. I told myself: 'You're not a machine. You're a human being. You're not always going to produce a perfect product.' Losses are important, too, Jasmine. The peaks aren't as high if you're always on top of them. You need the valleys, too. And from there, you build yourself up again."

"My problem is I tend to get stuck in the valleys."

"Do you? You can't allow yourself to stay there for long."

"Allow?" she said, making a face. "It's not that I allow it. I'm stuck. That's what being stuck means: You can't get out. That's the thing that you don't seem to understand, Katarina. Not everyone has the talent to get to the top like you. You can't just will yourself to be better than everyone else. Maybe I'm a third- or fourth-place skater. That's still pretty good, right? Third or fourth best in the whole country? Maybe that's as high as I'm ever going to get."

"Yes, that's possible. But at sixteen you're too young to know."

"What if I spend the next three years working my ass off and I'm still third or fourth? When am I not too young to know? At twenty? At twenty-one? Who's going to tell me? Will you?"

I smiled. "I'll send you an e-mail."

"That'd be swell. Meanwhile, I've wasted my life."

"Don't talk nonsense. Even if what you fear is true, that you're never going to get higher than third or fourth, it's the journey that makes it worthwhile, not the destination. Focus on the journey. When you try to strive for perfection in one area, you'll keep those habits forever. They're the same ones that will enable you to succeed in other areas of life. That's what makes sports worthwhile for everyone, not just the few who are champions."

"I wish I could believe that: That all those hours perfecting my layback spin will somehow magically translate into making me, say, a successful massage therapist. Or businesswoman. That just seems a little far-fetched."

"I don't think so. It's called discipline. It shows you can accept personal responsibility, which is useful in anything you pursue. I'm not saying there isn't a point when it's time to move on. There is. I've seen skaters who are satisfied finishing fifth or sixth and find a comfort level there. You don't want that. If you're not out there trying to win, I don't see the point. The whole idea is to force yourself beyond your comfort level."

"If you ask me, I'm already beyond it."

"I doubt it. I think you're in it. That's where you're stuck, if you're stuck anywhere. That's why Peter Meier wants you to go somewhere else to train. You'll know when you've gone as far as you can go, sweetie. It's not like a marathon. In skating, most girls technically peak when they're young, before their bodies have fully matured, when they can still spin fast enough in the air to do the jumps. But you're not there yet. You need to give yourself a couple more years of good honest effort."

Jasmine shrugged. She wasn't going to give in to me. "So how did we get back on my problems? You were telling me about your loss to Debi Thomas."

"All right. Yes, well of course I was quite upset right after the short program. I remember going into the dressing room crying and throwing my skate guards against the wall. I had Frau Müller beside me, which made me cry even more, because every loss was very dramatic to Frau Müller. She'd sit beside me and would try to smile, but beneath the smile she'd be gritting her teeth, asking, 'What was the matter? Why did you make a mistake?' She'd be smiling at me, but not really. You know this look? And without even knowing it she'd grab my leg and would dig her nails in."

"Yikes!"

"She'd just squeeze my thigh until it hurt. I'd be thinking: Owww. Owww. Owww. But I didn't say anything. I was pretty good about taking a loss. I didn't hold onto it for long. But it was always a big setback for Frau Müller, which was hard for me to deal with, because in the first place I was upset with myself. It would have been much better to have somebody comfort me at that point. Instead, Frau Müller would pound on my failure like someone banging on an anvil, making it even more painful. On the other hand, it doesn't really help to have somebody say, 'It's okay. Next time you'll be better,' when next time doesn't come for another year."

"Quelle bummer for you," Jasmine said.

I shrugged. "This is what happens when sport is used for political reasons," I said. "Your country uses you as a political tool in a way. You feel like the whole world is tumbling down around you. It's not just you who has lost. It's your country. It's your political system. You've let down everyone. That's how they make you feel. You'd come home and feel like a complete loser, even though you'd won a silver medal. Other people would be thrilled, just thrilled, to take that color medal home with them. But for me, I didn't win the silver—I'd lost the gold."

"Put me in the camp who would die for a silver in the Worlds."

"Sometimes I used to think: Maybe I should just kill myself and not come home. I'd be afraid, in a way. I'd really feel I'd failed. That feeling would only be there for a few hours, or at most a few days, but it would be intense. Frau Müller usually called me Kati. When she called me Katarina I knew something was wrong. So after a loss it would be: 'Katarina, come into my dressing room.' And I'd think: 'Uh-oh.' Then she'd verbally pound on me for half an hour, and I'd get smaller and smaller and smaller, like a little piece of nothing. 'Katarina, you've let me down and have disappointed all the people who've helped you. You didn't train hard enough. You put on too much weight. You've embarrassed me.' But then, slowly but surely, she'd start to build me back up, saying she believed in me. She wouldn't let me give up. She'd do whatever it took to get me back on top. And by the time it was over, you knew you were a champion. It's like the routine we had before I went out to skate. Every time, she'd put her hand on my hand on the boards, and she'd look at me and would say: 'You can do it, Kati. You are a champion. Just

ABOVE: Little me, at about 18 months. Are those the legs of a figure skater? (*Courtesy of the author*)

RIGHT: An early skating picture, with very skinny legs, 1979. (*Christoph Höhne*)

Me with my manager, business partner, and friend, Elisabeth Gottmann, who thought I might be able to help Jasmine. (*Courtesy Elisabeth Gottmann*)

LEFT: My first serious skating rival, Anett Pötzsch, with our mutual coach Frau Müller in 1976. Anett would be Olympic champion in 1980—and later my sister-in-law! (*Ullsteinbild/The Granger Collection, New York*)

ABOVE RIGHT: Me in the same dress, skating in my first European championship in Zagreb (former Yugoslavia), in 1979. We often didn't have money for new costumes in the GDR in those days, so they were passed from one girl to another. (*Courtesy of the author*)

RIGHT: My parents, Manfred and Kate. I left home before they wanted me to, but we became closer once I did. (*Courtesy of the author*)

LEFT: Skating my free program and winning my first European title in Dortmund, West Germany, in 1983. (*Arthur A. Werner*)

RIGHT: Winning my first Olympic gold medal, in Sarajevo, 1984. (*Interfoto/LOOKback/ Rainer Martini*)

Doing the last spin in my free program, "Maria," at the Cincinnati world championships in 1987, thinking: "Yes, yes, yes! I hope the judges give me great marks . . ." (*Courtesy of the author*)

Frau Müller and I react to a surprise 6.0 after my free program in Cincinnati. I won the title back from Debi Thomas. (*Courtesy of the author*)

We had to add feathers to the bottom of this costume, which I wore for the short program at the Calgary '88 Olympics, after my rival Elizabeth Manley's coach complained that I was "exploiting myself" and that "we're here to skate in a dress, not a G-string." Those comments made me even more happy to win. (*Interfoto/LOOKback/ Rainer Martini*)

On the podium in 1988 with silver medalist Elizabeth Manley and my rival Carmen, bronze medalist Debi Thomas. Debi wouldn't shake my hand on the podium, which upset people, but I actually admired her for it. Her dream had been shattered, she did not feel glad for me, and she was honest about it. (*AP/Wide World Photos*)

Carmen again! Here I played her in my Emmy Award–winning HBO special, *Carmen on Ice*, in 1990. (*Dino Ricci*)

Filming the last scene of *Carmen on Ice* with Brian Boitano on Christmas Eve in Berlin. While I am sad to "die," he can't wait to get off the ice and catch a plane to make it home in time for Christmas. (*Courtesy of the author*)

The short program at the 1994 Olympics in Lillehammer. Even though it was technically against the rules, I skated in tights because I refused to play Robin Hood running through the forest in a skirt. (*AP/Wide World Photos*)

Skating my long program at Lillehammer to "Where Have All the Flowers Gone," my tribute to Sarajevo in the midst of its horrible civil war. I started my Olympic comeback wanting only to skate to that song and carry that message to the Olympic stage, and then got sidetracked by thinking I could medal. (*AP/Wide World Photos*)

The way you practice is the secret to success. Frau Müller, now in her 70s, still makes me work harder than I'd work on my own.
(*Photos Gosbert Gottmann, www.lagalerie.de*)

go out there and do it. Show the world you're the best.' She was good in that way. She could really motivate you. And when you got back home to start training again after a loss, she was always supportive. Then you'd start from scratch."

"What does 'start from scratch' mean?"

"In terms of preparation. When you have a setback like I did in 1986, you have to put some thought into every aspect of your training. Are you working hard enough? Are you in good enough shape? Because it was true I was sometimes lazy, especially in the summer, when I didn't take my workout routine seriously. But I always knew what it took to get in shape when it really mattered. So you try not to overanalyze things. You accept what happened and put it behind you. Okay, it happened. There's nothing to be done about it now. But you also try to take some strength and energy from your setbacks. I told myself I'd be better next year. I'd train harder. That's why the next two years I really worked hard on my compulsory figures, even though I hated them, because now I had the motivation: to win my title back. I always had a very positive energy about things, this inner voice that was telling me: 'Everything will work out.' I never left a competition thinking I'd lost for any other reason than my mistakes. I never thought someone else won because they were better. Or because the judges blew it. It was because I didn't deliver. If I'd delivered, I would have won."

"You never thought the judges blew it? It seems like the judges are always blowing it in our sport."

I shrugged. "I understood early on that the judging was imperfect. But Frau Müller always said if you don't give the judges a chance to deduct, you're going to win eventually. There's nothing else they can do. You have to go into a competition with the attitude that you will perform so well no judge can do anything except put you first. Give them nothing to deduct."

"Do you like this new code of points judging? Or do you miss the old 6.0 system?"

"Figure skating will never have a judging system that's completely fair, but the new one they've put in is a start, and the rules force you to become a better skater. When you choose a sport like skating, you have to accept that it's a difficult sport to judge. But it's judgeable. The artistry's the hardest. One judge says, 'I like his style.' And the next says, 'Oh, no. It's too dramatic. I want something energetic.' Personal opinions will always be part of judging. It's just something you have to accept when you get into the sport. In the old 6.0 system, judges tended to go with their feelings. And that was part of what created excitement for the audience. They could complain and boo and whistle if they didn't like a judge's decision. The main thing I really don't like about the new code of points system is it's too sterile. It's so unemotional. The audience looks up and sees a bunch of decimal points. It might tell them the placements of the skaters, but somehow it comes across as impersonal and cold. They're just numbers. For whatever reason, I was more emotionally attached to the 5.8s and 5.9s and the rare 6.0s than the scores I'm seeing now, and I think the audience feels the same thing. Skating is a sport that needs the audience to be emotionally involved. The other thing I don't like about the new system is that the judges are anonymous to the skaters and the audience. You can't point to the scores and say, 'Why didn't you give me more?' It's good for the judges, because they don't feel pressured. But they should be held responsible for what they do."

"No kidding," Jasmine said. "Do they judge differently at the Olympics than at other competitions?"

"At the Olympics, they always judge the moment. The gold medal is decided on the emotions of the moment. If you look back on the last three Olympics, it's happened every time. Oksana Baiul won in 1994, Tara Lipinski in 1998, and Sarah Hughes in 2002. All of them won by the emotional power of their performances that night, not because of what they'd done their whole career. Sarah was the best on every level: technical and emotional. She delivered her performance in such a fresh, young, innocent way. Which is what Tara did, too. But a judge can be impressed and fooled at the same time. Oksana won in Lillehammer because her skating touched people that night. She was very much this poor Ukrainian orphan. She'd had an accident the day before, where her calf was cut in a collision in practice with Tanja Szewczenko, and everyone's heart just went out to her. When you look back now at the performance on tape, it's clear that Nancy Kerrigan, who finished second, deserved to win. She somehow has to live with that the rest of her life. She skated a great free program technically, very athletic, very clean, but her performance was not very passionate. She was somewhat reserved. Oksana, on the other hand, made several mistakes in her program. She two-footed some jumps. But the judges, and the spectators, too, went with their emotions. They got it wrong, but that's the way our sport is. If you don't like it, pack up your things and do something else. Go run. Sometimes it's not just the athletic side that counts, it's the emotional side."

Jasmine turned the page of the scrapbook, and I saw a headline that mentioned Cincinnati. That was the city where the World Championships were held in 1987, and the place where I skated what was probably the best program of my life. Certainly it was my favorite Worlds.

"I had such an accent back then when I spoke English," I said, laughing. "I remember my friend Judy Blumberg was interviewing me on TV, and she asked what I was doing in Ohio. I said: 'I've come to Chin-chin-ati to win my title back.' That was the clip the stations replayed all week."

It was an unforgettable experience, and as Jasmine paused to look at the pictures from one of the magazine stories I'd brought home, I told her about that week in Cincinnati. Not only were the performances attended by standing-room-only crowds, the practices were usually packed with 3,000–4,000 people. And whenever my name was announced, the American audiences always applauded and cheered. I was amazed by that. Debi's coach, Alex McGowan, even complained that I was milking the crowds at practices by acknowledging their applause with waves and smiles. He came out in the newspapers and asked them not to fall for it and to be more nationalistic. It made Frau Müller so mad. She told some reporters that we were just trying to keep good public relations, and part of skating is to smile and bow to people when they clap. Fortunately, the audiences remained just as polite afterward. They were patriotic toward their own skaters, but they totally respected other athletes as well. They just loved to watch skating.

I was in great shape, weighing 115 pounds—nine pounds less than I had a year earlier in Geneva. But the competition didn't start very well for me. I finished fifth in the compulsory figures, three places behind Debi, which meant I could win both the short and the long programs and still finish behind her overall, as long as she finished second in both those events. But Debi hadn't been skating as well that year. She'd been beaten in the U.S. Championships by Jill Trenary and had had a problem all season with tendinitis in her foot. In the short program, which I won, she made a mistake on her double axel and finished seventh. So, going into the free-skating program it was Kira Ivanova of the Soviet Union in first; I was in second; and Debi Thomas was in third. Whoever won the long would be world champion.

I always liked skating last, because you knew exactly what you had to do to win. The people who skated earlier had to set the bar in terms of quality, and sometimes—I don't know why—weak skating was followed by weak skating. So I liked it when the skaters before me skated well. That meant I had to be better and stronger. If they made mistakes, you couldn't help but think: 'Maybe now I can make a mistake, too.' It's human nature. You'd pull back a little bit. You wouldn't be as aggressive. You'd think: 'I've got room for error.' Which is wrong, of course. You shouldn't let what others are doing affect you. You never have room for error. That was the lesson I learned in Copenhagen back in 1982. So it was better when the skaters before me were flawless, because then you had no choice except to be perfect.

Frau Müller referred to the arena in Cincinnati as a "witch's kettle" because the stands rose so steeply from the ice. It seated more than 15,000 people and was the loudest building I can remember. I drew the next-to-last spot, and Debi was just before me, which was perfect.

Backstage was like when you go to the circus, and you see the tigers prowling around each other. That's how it felt warming up. We all watched each other out of the corners of our eyes, but not really. It's like when you stare through someone. We felt like wild animals in the circus, pacing in our cages, waiting to be let into the ring.

All the girls in the last group skated incredibly, and as I waited, each got better and better. There was Elizabeth Manley, then Caryn Kadavy, then Debi, then me. Kira Ivanova was last. Debi was amazing. She landed five triple jumps and two double axels, all flawless, and skated at the highest level. I came out thirty seconds before her ending, and her coach was already jumping up and down. I could see on her face she did really, really well, so I knew I had to beat the best and give more than I ever gave in practice. It sounded like a thunderstorm of applause when she left the ice. Flowers rained down, and someone even handed her a pizza.

Then it was up to me. As I waited for the crowd to settle down, I noticed Debi standing at the side of the rink. She was going to wait and watch my free program. On top of everything else, that gave me the extra kick I needed. Watching her, I was thinking: "Now I'm going to show you what I can do."

It was everything I loved: fierce competition, performing for an audience, skating. I've never experienced an audience like the one in Cincinnati. Debi was their own champion, their darling, but when they announced my name, the audience also clapped like crazy for me. That happens rarely in a country that's not your own. You could tell they were real skating fans. And after I was done, it was a thunderstorm for me, as well. Frau Müller later said she'd seen me do that *West Side Story* program a hundred times, but that day it was as if she'd seen it for the first time. It was the best I ever skated. I even did a triple loop, which I often left out if I didn't need it. I was always very diplomatic about which jumps I'd use, and that was my hardest jump. But I knew I needed everything on that night.

When I won, I felt total gratification. Afterward someone asked Debi about my performance, and she was extremely gracious. "This was sort of a test to see how tough she was," Debi said. "Well, she's really tough. I just said to myself, 'The girl's amazing.'"

That meant a lot to me. At the time people were always talking about how flirtatious I was with the audiences and judges. They never mentioned my toughness and athleticism. I suppose they did it in a complimentary way: "All Katarina has to do is step on the ice and she's won their hearts!" Which was great in a way. But I wanted people to perceive me as an athlete. I wanted them to know I won because I was the best. Debi honored me with her comment, and I haven't forgotten it.

It wasn't the last time Debi honored me, incidentally. I'll never forget that at my very last professional competition, in the fall of 2000, of all the judges on the panel it was Debi Thomas who gave me my highest marks.

10

Calgary Olympics, 1988

Debi Thomas and I did battle again less than a year later, at the 1988 Olympics in Calgary. As if the rivalry wasn't intense enough, we both chose to do our long programs to music from the opera *Carmen*.

I found out Debi was skating to *Carmen* early in the fall, from a Canadian fan who used to send me tapes of early season competitions in North America. One of the tapes showed Debi's long program, and I couldn't believe that of all the music out there to choose from, we'd both taken selections from the same opera. I watched the tape with Frau Müller, and afterward we looked at each other and said: "Well, there's really nothing to worry about. We have the better Carmen."

I was really confident of that. Debi's music was probably the most exciting from the opera, very fast and spirited, but she was not portraying Carmen as a character. She used the more joyful theme and just skated. I'd chosen music from the most dramatic scene, the one where Carmen is killed by her jealous lover, which I believed to be much more intriguing. I always loved skating to Spanish music, with its wonderful rhythm, style, and characters. The women are very proud, and they use that evocative body language I adore.

You hear people say today that much of the glamour has gone out of figure skating. When I skated I always played dramatic, larger-than-life characters and wore theatrical costumes. The great thing about skating, to me, is it's really a cross between sports and entertainment. I tried to bring to singles skating what a lot of the best ice dancers were doing back then: telling a story on the ice.

No one in singles skating really portrayed characters in their programs until I started doing it. That became my trademark. In my amateur career I played Mozart, Maria from *West Side Story*, Robin Hood, and Carmen. I also played a night club dancer while skating to Glenn Miller's "In the Mood." We didn't just take a piece of music and add choreography. We came up with this original concept of playing a character, because we always felt like the underdogs, coming from East Germany, a country people thought of as dark and miserable, with no fun and no freedom. So we had to be different, better, more creative. We had to be special in a way other skaters were not. We brought in a costume designer from the theater in East Berlin, so my costumes weren't skating costumes. They were character costumes: Hungarian, Oriental, Spanish, Viennese. It was all very innovative. And for all of that, too, I give credit to Frau Müller.

Getting the *Carmen* program prepared, I'd frustrated my choreographer all season. He was a Czech, Rudi Suchy, and he'd worked with me and developed my programs for many years. I had to be in character for all four minutes of my program. Carmen is very flirtatious, a free and independent woman, who only wanted to live her life to the fullest. The man who loved her was extremely jealous, and he finally killed her. So it's quite a dramatic story. I'd been pretty emotionless in practice throughout the season, and Mr. Suchy would go crazy because I wasn't doing his choreography right. "Be seductive," he'd shout. "You should be flirting!" And I'd go, "Why? It's empty in here." I was ashamed, alone on the ice, flirting to empty walls and a few coaches. I needed an audience to do it right. I didn't mind performing for 10,000 people, but I couldn't turn on the electricity for a few bare walls.

I wasn't worried, though. I was always better in competition than I was at practice, and I knew that once I got in front of an audience, I'd become Carmen, portraying the character with all the emotion and passion it called for. Plus I'd been to an Olympics. I'd won the gold medal. I knew what I was going to be in for, and that all eyes would be on me and my rivalry with Debi, especially since I had the chance to be only the second woman to win back-to-back Olympics, after Sonja Henie. I definitely felt more pressure on me the second time, because my performance would also have an affect on my professional career. My government had made me a deal that if I brought home a second gold medal, I could skate the next year with Holiday on Ice, which was the European version of Ice Capades. I'd be the special guest star on a five-city tour. Of course, the government would send an official with me, to make sure I didn't defect, but it was still a chance to travel and see the world. It was a chance to perform before audiences, which is what I really loved to do. So as far as I was concerned, my future depended on winning.

It became known as The Battle of the Carmens, and the interest in it built and built during the early days of the Olympics. The American press loved the contrast we presented: Debi, the black, athletic champion from the United States, who attended Stanford and wanted to be a doctor, against the defending champion, the artistic beauty from the repressive German Democratic Republic. I had so many requests for interviews I couldn't accommodate them all, so I held a press conference beforehand, which was the first time the International Olympic Committee had ever done that for someone in figure skating.

In Calgary there never seemed to be enough hours in the day. As was the case in Sarajevo, I missed Opening Ceremonies and never got to see any of the other Olympic competitions. My days were filled with workouts, training, massage, and meals. I watched some of the events on television, but I couldn't really enjoy them. I never really enjoyed the Olympic experience as a sporting event until Lillehammer in 1994, and that was at a completely different point in my career.

Compulsory figures in Calgary went very, very well. I finished third, just behind Debi, who was second. I was so nervous I threw up afterward. It had never happened before, but Frau Müller said, "Don't worry. It's only nerves." The compulsories were what I was most afraid of, because one tiny little wobble could cost you the title. And when you're nervous and you're shaking in figures, the judges can tell by the line your blade leaves on the ice. It wiggles. Fortunately, all the work I'd done in figures that year paid off, and my nervousness didn't show on the outside. It was one of my best compulsory figures ever. The worst part was now behind me.

Still, there was controversy. Liz Manley, the Canadian champion, had a coach named Peter Dunfield, who during the Olympics accused me of "exploiting" myself because of the costume I planned to wear for the short program. He said it was more suited for a circus and that "all that's missing is the horse and reins. We're here to skate in a dress, not in a G-string."

The costume was cut high at the hips to show off my legs, but by today's standards it was nothing unusual or special. The complaint was part of a pattern that had emerged in the previous couple of years, where other coaches accused me of winning because of my looks instead of my talent. Things weren't helped when the German magazine *Sports International* chose February to publish the photo they'd taken of me at the Paris exhibition in October, the one with my boob popping out of my dress. That magazine was making the rounds in skating circles in Calgary. So rather than risk offending any judges, Frau Müller had our costume designer add some feathers to the bottom of my blue showgirl costume before the short program. I skated well in it and won, but Debi, who finished second in the short, was in first place going into the long program. Whichever Carmen the judges liked better would win the gold.

I've never felt such pressure before a competition. It seemed like the whole world was watching, and most of America was. The Battle of the Carmens drew television ratings that were enormous, trailing only a few Super Bowls among sports telecasts at the time.

It's funny to look back on, because everyone said afterward how remarkable my makeup was for Carmen: "Oh my God, that was so dramatic! We've never seen you look this way before, Katarina!" That was certainly true, but it wasn't anything Frau Müller and I had planned. It was because I was so frickin' nerv-

ous I kept running into the bathroom and putting on makeup
before I skated. I'd warm up in the hallway, then I'd go back
into the dressing room and put on some more eye shadow.
Warm up some more . . . put on more lipstick. Warm up some
more . . . put on more rouge. Out of nervousness, I just kept ap-
plying makeup. The good thing was that it went with the red-
and-black costume and the Spanish-theme program. But, my
God, I ended up with the darkest eyes.

Right before I went out, I have lots of pictures of me yawning.
People thought I was so relaxed, even bored, but nothing could
have been further from the truth. I was yawning because I
needed more oxygen. Luckily, in free skating you can hide your
nervousness by moving, by jumping around and spinning, keep-
ing your body in constant motion. That's what I tried to do in
Calgary, to keep aggressive, but I wasn't perfect. I only did four
of my planned five triples, leaving out the loop. But I enjoyed
the program. I really got into the character. My choreographer
was probably out there biting the boards, wondering where that
had been all year. The only frustrating thing was that I was
never able to show my joy. After I doubled the triple loop, I was
of course disappointed, but it was at a sad part in the music, so it
was fine for me to look sad. Then I landed a triple salchow, and
a triple toe, but I wasn't allowed to show how happy that made
me! I had to stay in character. I couldn't go into the last move
smiling and laughing, because in the next moment I would be
dead, stabbed by my jealous lover.

As I lay on the ice in my death throes, I knew I hadn't been
perfect. I knew the door was now open for Debi. So I was a little
sad in what turned out to be a moment of triumph. That's why I
prefer to skate last. Everything at that moment was uncertain.

So I was bowing and smiling, but thinking: "Dumkoff! Why didn't you do the loop, the loop, the loop?!"

After my marks came up, I sat in the stands to watch Debi, who skated next. Frau Müller wasn't with me. She'd already left. She was upset because she knew I'd left the door open. I was never happy about the way she didn't stay with me. I can understand it, though. She didn't tolerate mistakes.

Frau Müller and I always followed a routine in the moments before I skated—I'd always put my hand in her hand—and in the same way, Debi and her coach, Alex McGowan, had a routine. After Mr. McGowan gave her some final words of encouragement while standing at the side of the boards, they'd exchange two-handed high fives. They'd slap both palms together every time. Only this time, she missed. They hit air. And from that moment, I knew she wouldn't win. She wasn't there. She was afraid. I could see it. By that time I'd developed a knowledge about her as a competitor, where I could see in her eyes and her body language how she'd perform, and I knew then she was off. And human nature being what it is, I began thinking: 'Fall, fall, fall!' Everybody does it. I'll be honest about it. You sit on your hands and think: 'Please fall on your trunks.' You try to be as emotionless as possible, but inside, when they fall, you're like: YESSS!!!!

And sure enough, Debi missed her first combination, which was a triple toe, triple toe—a very difficult jump. That's when I knew I should win. Then, disheartened, she started making other mistakes, and it was clear to me she'd started to give up. She looked like she wanted to leave the ice. Debi missed three triple jumps in all, which was very uncharacteristic, and she ended up finishing third, behind Liz Manley. I honestly felt sorry for her.

When we were on the podium, Debi never gave me her hand to congratulate me. At one point I held my hand out to her, but she totally ignored me, and the whole world saw it. People were so upset. But I didn't think anything about it, honestly. Everyone else thought it was bad sportsmanship, but I understood. Leading after the short program, she expected to win, or at the worst to be second. And her whole country was expecting her to win. Now she was third, and she was completely crushed. Her dream had been shattered. I thought, "At least she was honest." I admired that. I liked that in her. I still admire her.

Afterward Carlo Fassi, the famous American figure-skating coach who was originally from Italy, brought the Italian skiing champion Alberto Tomba backstage to meet me. Tomba had won two gold medals and had been the most exciting man in the Calgary Games. He was wearing his medals, but I didn't know who he was. As an East German figure skater, I never met any skiers or hockey players. Why should I have known him? I was thinking, "Who's that running around the skating arena with two gold medals? Definitely not a skater." So when Carlo introduced us, I asked him, in English: "In which sport did you win these gold medals?"

It was innocent enough, but I think Tomba felt like someone had shot him in the head. He's this huge Italian macho star, and he wanted to meet me, but he couldn't speak one word of English. And I hadn't a clue who he was. Nor could I have cared less at that particular moment.

At the press conference afterward I started giggling and couldn't stop, because I'd had a few beers before my doping test so I could pee. I never drank alcohol, so it was enough to make me tipsy, and I started playing with the two little Olympic mascots while answering questions in English. I spoke only a little at the time, having learned from lessons I'd taken at school. But mostly I'd learned on the tour from other skaters. It was enough to communicate, and the press liked that, since I was one of the few East German athletes who spoke any English at all. Our sports officials encouraged me to speak it, because they understood figure skating was a different sport than, say, running. They knew you had to be nice to judges, and that skating has social elements to it that the other sports don't have. It's important that the judges like you. That's figure skating. You're not always judged on what you do on the ice, and what they see. Maybe one judge likes a blonde more than a brunette, so as a brunette you've already lost.

The World Championships the next month were in Budapest, which is where I won my fourth and final Worlds title. I did the Tom Collins tour afterward, the one he calls Champions on Ice. I had special permission from the government to do it. After the last show in Las Vegas, I remember we were sitting in a suite with Brian Orser, Brian Boitano, the Canadian ice dancers Tracy Wilson and Rob McCall, and the Russian ice dancers Natalia Bestimiova and Andre Bukin, and we were so sad we were crying. We'd all become great friends over the years, and we were thinking we might never see each other in this world again, because there weren't the opportunities in skating then that there soon would be. There was still an East and West Germany separated by a massive impenetrable wall. Nobody dreamed it would come down so fast. And my government, which had allowed me to tour with the Holiday on Ice in Europe, would never have let me come back for a full tour of America. It was too far away. And for the East German sports officials, sport was supposed to be amateur, even though they paid us bonuses and organized us so professionally. You were not supposed to be able to make a living on it for the rest of your life, that's for sure.

I always thought we, as athletes, were more advanced than our politicians. The Cold War between the countries of the East and the West didn't exist among the skaters. We got along. We were friends. We didn't sit around trying to prove who had the better system. When we'd go on tour, we'd sit in one room, an East German, a Canadian, a Russian, a West German, and an American, and you couldn't help but wonder: Why can't the politicians just sit at a table like this?

Still, I was protected and watched over by Frau Müller. She'd let me go out and have a good time with the other skaters, but she kept an eye on me. She didn't like me to be too friendly with the girls I had to compete against. And I never was. It was always my nature to be better friends with the pairs skaters and ice dancers, and the men's singles skaters, than the girls I had to try to beat once the tour ended. I had May through September to get prepared for a new season and into a competitive frame of mind. To forget that the girls I competed against were ever my friends.

Now that I'm older, of course, I realize that in skating you're really just competing against yourself. The other skaters . . . the judges . . . they're not things you can control. It should be just about you and your skating. You know when you've performed well. As an athlete, you don't need the judges to tell you that.

But I'm in another stage of my life. When I was an amateur, I couldn't have thought that way and been a two-time Olympic champion. I had to think of the other girls as my opponents, not as my friends.

11

Celebrity Dinners

Jasmine was seated on the floor of my study, the scrapbooks strewn around her in a semicircle. I knelt on a pillow beside her. She started to reach for the next book, the one on the 1994 Olympics in Lillehammer, but I stopped her.

"Let's take a break," I said. "We'll save that one for tomorrow. Aren't you getting hungry?"

"I've lost complete track of time."

"I'd like to take you to dinner at my favorite Berlin restaurant. It's the place I went to with Jack Nicholson."

"The actor? Oh my God."

"The one and only."

"Did you date him?"

"It was just a dinner. But it was so funny. He was in Berlin last year for the film festival, which is where he chose to open

Something's Gotta Give, the movie he made costarring Diane Keaton. Berlin has picked up a lot of festivals and trade fairs recently, and this was a very big deal. Almost like the Oscars night in Hollywood. One of the newspapers interviewed me about it, and I mentioned I thought Jack Nicholson was an incredible actor. His publicist, Pat Kingsley, who used to be my publicist as well, read it in the paper and spent the next day tracking me down. It turns out Jack Nicholson had seen me skate in New York's Madison Square Garden with his kids, and Pat told me he wanted to take me to dinner."

"That is so awesome. I'd have died."

"So I told him about Borchardt, which is the restaurant we'll go to tonight. It's great food, and it's really the place to go in Berlin for celebrities to see and be seen. Not just movie people, but athletes, businessmen, politicians, actors. It's very difficult to get into during the film festival, but I go there a lot and can always get a table. For that night, I reserved two of them: One in a private corner and one in the most central location. I thought I would let him choose. So I arrived and was sitting with the publicist, and fifteen minutes later in walked Jack Nicholson, like a gunfighter walking into a saloon. He came in the back entrance, and every eye was on him. They were wondering who he was going to meet, and what a nice feeling to know he was coming to MY table! They were all so jealous. He sat down and the first thing I said to him was what I'd told Elisabeth earlier that day. 'Oh my God, the devil wants to meet me.' He looked at me with that smile he uses in the movies, the one where one eyebrow goes up, and he said: 'You are so-o-o right.'"

Jasmine gave a delighted squeal. "You said that? 'The devil wants to meet me?'"

"Yes. And he answered, 'You are so-o-o right.' It was such fun. We had a three-hour meal. There were about twenty-five photographers outside the front of the restaurant trying to get a picture of us, but Rainer, the maître d', wouldn't let them in. It was a sensation to have him there. When we finished, we left by the back entrance, and he offered me his car and driver, who drove me home while Jack walked back to his hotel. It was a thoroughly delightful evening."

"What was he like?"

"Really just the way he is in the movies. Very fun and entertaining. When you see him in *Something's Gotta Give*, you definitely think he's playing himself."

"I saw that. He looked pretty old."

I laughed. "Well, he's still got what it takes, I can tell you that. He is so funny. He admitted that unfortunately he'd fallen asleep before I skated in the Stars on Ice show in Madison Square Garden. But what a life he leads! I was laughing about it during dinner, but I was also thinking, 'Oh my God, this is nuts, having a huge crowd of photographers waiting outside the restaurant for you.' That happens to him all the time. Luckily for me, I have a lower profile. I can live a life that's somewhat normal. I can walk around Berlin and not be bothered by people."

She clapped her hands and grinned. "Did he hit on you?"

I pursed my lips in a mock pout. "Oh, no. He was a perfect gentleman, I promise."

"I'll bet he did."

"No, no. Though actors do love athletes. One thing I learned when I lived in Los Angeles was American movie stars have tremendous respect for athletes. So when I meet someone like him, or Tom Cruise, or Robert DeNiro, I feel I'm meeting them on the same level. Movie stars want to be athletes, and athletes want to be movie stars. We share a mutual envy."

"When did you meet Tom Cruise?"

"I was in his movie *Jerry Maguire*. Did you see it? He played a sports agent and I played myself. A very brief cameo."

"I've never seen it, but now I'm going to rent it."

"My poster, which was on the wall of Jerry Maguire's office, was in the movie longer than I was. But it was fun. Everyone was so nice, and they all knew who I was because of the Olympics."

"I've been wondering, I mean, this may sound stupid, but do you ever get tired of being famous? Does it ever get to you?"

"That's not a silly question." I thought for a moment before answering further. Fame was something I'd lived with so long I hardly remembered what it was like not to be recognized in public. "There are positive and negative sides to it," I said. "The bad thing is, you can't do anything in the public eye without being judged. They judge the way you talk, the way you dress. And it's impossible to keep a secret you'd like to hide. These days, everything comes out. There are journalists around taking pictures, waiting outside your door. Like in the movie *Notting Hill*. On the other hand, it's nice to be able to call a restaurant ten minutes before you leave and to get your favorite table. It's nice to be pampered when you go out. It's nice when strangers come up and tell you they love what you do."

"And to be invited to all those parties and festivals with famous actors."

"Yes, that too," I smiled. "But you know, Jasmine, I only accept maybe 5 percent of the invitations I get, and most are not any fun. They're work. You try to decide what's an important event and who else will be there. You can't overexpose yourself.

And then when you do go out, everything has to be perfect. So I hire somebody to do my hair and makeup. It takes two hours. You don't just wake up and look glamorous. Because always there will be photographers, and you have to look beautiful. And you need the right clothes, the right outfits, the right shoes. And you need several of them, because once you wear a beautiful dress that's seen on TV, you can never wear it again. Otherwise people will say, 'Poor Katarina, she doesn't make any money. She has to wear her dress twice.' It's true, Jasmine. I swear to you. People watch for things like that. So you get a store to lend the outfits to you. I don't want my closets filled with clothes."

"Who lends you clothes?"

"I get mine from designer Rena Lange of Munich, or Escada, or some other designer. I go there for the day, and then I pick out different outfits. Then I take them back and exchange them for the next season. The whole celebrity thing is like a job. You do it to stay in the public eye. But if you want to really have quality time, you should just go with friends to dinner, dress very casually, and laugh. Which is what we'll do tonight. Okay?"

"Okay. I don't have to put on a fancy outfit?"

"Not if you don't wish to. I'm just wearing slacks. I'll call Uwe, my friend from downstairs, and see if he can join us. He's from Chemnitz."

"I'll just quickly change into something a little nicer."

"Let's be ready to go in a half hour. I'll call the restaurant and see if they can put us at my usual table. We might even see someone famous!" I added with a twinkle in my eye.

Something of a change was coming over Jasmine. She seemed more upbeat, more engaged in the world I was sharing with her. I began to think that maybe the time we were spending together might be doing her some good, after all.

I knew she'd like Uwe Kästner, who was my oldest friend, someone I'd known for more than twenty years. Uwe and I grew up together in Chemnitz. He'd been an archer, and his mother had been a doctor at my sports club. We'd played tennis together as youngsters. Now he was an orthopedic doctor, very handsome, who was so relaxed about life, so open to differing points of view, I sometimes wanted to strangle him. "Make a stand!" I wanted to scream. "Tell me what you really think!" He rented one of the apartments downstairs, which he shared with Clint, the dancer who worked at the health facility we'd been to that afternoon. Between the two of them, they kept me up to date on Berlin's thriving cultural scene.

Uwe's unbelievably tolerant, which is one of the things I've learned from him: to respect other people for what they are and to accept in them what you cannot change. We'll go to the ballet together or to some modern dance company's performance, and if I don't like it, I'll want to leave. Uwe will say, "Why do you leave? Those are artists, and they're trying to express themselves. If you don't like it, that's your problem. You have to respect what they do."

I'll say to him, "Why? I rarely go and see dance performances, and if I take two hours of my precious time to do so, I want to get something out of it. I want to enjoy it. I don't want to get upset." Then he'll go: "Yep, but maybe that's what the artists wanted. They wanted to get you emotionally involved. They wanted to get a reaction, and that's a reaction." And I'll throw up my hands and say, "Oh, just leave me alone."

I understand what he means. Still, I'll leave.

He's the same way with people, and he tells me all the time to respect other people for what they are. If I bitch about somebody, he'll say to me: "Why complain? You can't change him. Respect the way he is, and worry about improving yourself." Sometimes Uwe is so dispassionate and analytical he comes across as emotionless, because he never complains about anything. But at the end of the day, he's always there for me. I can call him in the middle of the night about anything, and he'll listen. It helps more than I can tell you to have a friend like that.

Jasmine and I stopped to pick him up on the way downstairs, and we ended up having a glass of wine while waiting for Clint to get out of the shower. Then the four of us took my car to the restaurant. Borchardt is on Französische Strasse, a quiet street that runs parallel to Unter den Linden Strasse, the most famous boulevard in Berlin. As I drove, Uwe told Jasmine a little about its history. In 1647, the avenue was planted with walnut trees and linden trees, but the walnut trees died, and the lindens flourished, which is how the street got its name. Unter den Linden is where giant sports sculptures were erected during the 1936 Berlin Olympic Games, and where the Nazis staged their infamous book-burning bonfire outside the Old Library in May 1933. Humboldt University is on Unter den Linden, which is where Karl Marx studied; where Albert Einstein lectured; and where Max Planck revolutionized modern physics by working out his quantum physics theory. A huge statue of Frederick the Great (Frederick II of Prussia) on horseback stands in the center of the boulevard, positioned in such a way that it seems the kaiser has ridden from the Brandenburg Gate, the most famous landmark in Berlin, with its six Greek columns topped by a four-horse chariot driven by the goddess of victory. The Berlin Wall, which divided East from West Berlin from 1961 to 1989, used to stand just west of the Brandenburg Gate, and since its dismantling Unter den Linden has been a magnet for investment: world-class hotels, restaurants, cafés, and high-end retail stores. When the weather's nice, it's a wonderful boulevard for people-watching and shopping, and I have often walked there to absorb the rich history of Berlin's past. It's all around you, compelling, dramatic, poignant, and more than a little sad.

I love the city. Where I live, in Berlin Mitte, I have everything I could possibly need. Berlin, they say, is like a little New York, with the advantage that it's not nearly as expensive. It's the only city in Germany that's a melting pot of cultures—one big town created out of many little towns. Students, young people, artists, musicians, politicians, and businessmen all live there. Now the government is based there, housed in the glass-domed, reconstructed Reichstag Building, and some corporate headquarters are moving back. The architecture is bold and exciting. The ethnic restaurants are incredible. What used to be East Berlin has attracted most of the new investment, so that's where the trendiest places are.

I moved to Berlin late in the summer of 1988 to attend acting school, and to get out of Chemnitz, which held no future for me. Careerwise, this was the best place to be. My first apartment was right next to the wall. It actually looked over the wall, into the Tiergarten, which is like New York's Central Park, only with more trees. I read somewhere there used to be over 200,000 trees in the Tiergarten, but only 700 survived the war. Berlin was bombed to rubble. The park was reforested afterward by donations of beech trees from all over Germany, so now when you're there you forget you're in a city at all. The dirt and gravel paths in it are perfect for running. And once the wall came down, the park was just 200 yards from my door.

I chose that location in 1988 because I knew it would be quiet. The area near the wall was called "no-man's-land," and from my apartment window I looked down upon the "Death Strip"—the open, overgrown tract of land between the two walls the GDR had built, topped by barbed wire, to keep citizens from escaping to the West.

Little did I know that once the wall came down, in November 1989, I'd suddenly be living in the busiest place in the city, where most of the new construction projects were being built. But by then I had no desire to move. Around my neighborhood, new buildings began popping up like mushrooms after a rain. In the next decade five new office buildings went up between my apartment and Potsdamer Platz, which was just a few blocks away. The futuristic glass-and-steel Sony Center was built at Potsdamer Platz, a city within a city, with theaters, restaurants, an Imax cinema, hotels, condos, a shopping center. Over 5 billion euros were poured into it. I stayed because wanted to see the changes. I wanted to be part of it, to see how this divided city would grow back together. I didn't want to miss a thing.

Well, that's not quite the truth. I did want to miss the Love Parade, the annual bacchanalia that paralyzes Berlin every summer, a festival that attracts over a million young ravers to the Tiergarten. It's a week of sex, dancing, drinking, drugs, and rock and roll. People walk around naked and have sex beneath the beech trees, and the entire park turns yellow from everyone peeing on the grass. Rock bands play on the steps of the Victory Column, which is at the rotary axis between East and West

Berlin, the monument that stands 220 feet high and is topped by a golden-winged goddess thirty feet tall. I habitually fled when the Love Parade came to town. I always got as far away from Berlin as I could drive.

Jasmine, of course, was asking Uwe about it. All the young people from around Germany want to go to the Love Parade, which I admit brings millions and millions of dollars to the city. It's a rite of passage for German teens. I'd parked the car by this time, and we were just arriving at the restaurant, where my friend Rainer, the maître d', welcomed us at the door. "Katarina!" he said, hugging me. "Where have you been hiding?"

For me, coming into Borchardt is like walking into my living room. That's how much time I've spent there. Rainer's philosophy is to stay open until the last guest has left, and several times I had stayed there until three in the morning, wining and dining, long after the chairs had been placed on the tables and everyone else had gone home.

I introduced Jasmine, and Rainer, who never forgot a name, bowed deeply, then escorted us to my favorite table as the other diners watched to see who was worthy of these special attentions. He then brought us complimentary glasses of champagne, so right away it felt like we were having a party.

"What a treat," said Jasmine. "I could get used to this."

"I am used to it," Clint said with a chuckle. He was wearing a sleeveless fishnet shirt that had the table beside us staring slack-jawed. "Hang with Katarina. That's my motto. Living well's the best revenge."

"To living well," Uwe toasted. "Prosit."

"And to old friends," I added, sipping the champagne.

"And new ones," Uwe said, clinking Jasmine's glass.

She nodded in appreciation. "So you guys knew each other as kids?" she asked.

"As teenagers, anyway," I said. "In Chemnitz. Then we had a little separation as our lives took different paths. Uwe defected to the West. When was that? Two or three years before the Wall came down, yes? I think I was twenty years old."

"Something like that," Uwe said.

"My god. How did you defect?" Jasmine asked.

"Carefully," Uwe said, smiling.

"Really," she pursued. "We've studied that period in school, but I've never actually talked to someone who defected. How'd you get over the wall? Couldn't you have been shot?"

"In the trunk of a car, actually. So they wouldn't have shot me. Put me in jail, probably. It was pretty hairy."

He told her the story. Uwe had been going to medical school, and he and a friend decided they had to get to the West. It was nothing particular that set him off. Just general disaffection with the way of life.

Uwe knew the son of a Third World diplomat. This wild young man—let's call him Alan—had a tendency to live beyond his means, spending too much money on drugs, women, and alcohol. Uwe figured Alan would be willing to help them cross the border in exchange for a fee. With his diplomatic passport, Alan could cross from East to West and come back again whenever he liked. So Uwe offered him 10,000 marks to drive him and his friend to West Berlin in the trunk of a rental car.

Alan agreed. They'd heard the East German border guards had sensors that could detect the body heat of someone hiding in a trunk, so to test it out they made a trial run. They put a space heater in the trunk of the car and sent Alan through one of the checkpoints that had the least traffic. He made it without being searched, no problem. So now they were confident the plan would work and set the date for the escape.

Uwe's uncle had given him the money to pay for it, because 10,000 marks was a fortune by East German standards. His uncle and aunt lived in West Berlin. If Uwe made it across, that's where he was going to stay. Then Uwe had to make copies of his university transcripts, which was illegal, to show what courses he was taking. He needed them, because when he got to the West he wanted to resume his medical studies. He had decided not to tell his parents of his plans to defect, so afterward, when the police interviewed them, they could honestly swear they hadn't known what was coming. As the date of his escape approached, he simply told them he was going on holiday with a friend. When the day came, he said good-bye to his parents, rented a car with the last of his uncle's money, and waited with his friend for Alan to take them across. But Alan never showed.

Now they were in a bind. They had to return the rental car, go back home, and make up a story to tell their families about how their holiday had been canceled. In the next few days, Uwe tracked down Alan to learn what had gone wrong. Alan claimed he'd just forgotten the appointment, that he had no intention of running off with their money. So they set a new date for their escape. Only they were out of money, so Uwe and his friend had to steal from their parents in order to pay for the second rental car.

This time Alan showed up, though he was late and greatly agitated. He explained that he couldn't take them across because his father had sensed something was amiss and had locked his diplomatic passport in a strongbox. Uwe wasn't buying it. They had to leave tonight, he told Alan. This guy had taken their money and he was going to live up to his end of the bargain. "Show us the strongbox," Uwe demanded.

So the three of them sneaked into the diplomat's home, and using a hammer and screwdriver, Uwe broke into the strongbox. Sure enough, there was the passport. Alan was so nervous he was shaking uncontrollably, so Uwe gave him a prescription drug to calm his nerves. Then Alan decided he had to run away from home, too, having broken into his father's strongbox. So he hurriedly packed a suitcase and tossed it into the backseat of the rental. Uwe and his friend climbed into the trunk. As they lay there, listening as the car slowed as it neared the border checkpoint, Uwe started worrying the suitcase in the back seat would be a red flag. "Why not have the suitcase in the trunk?" the guards might wonder. He was also concerned the sedative he had given Alan would cause him to drive erratically. Or that he might talk crazily or pass out from the stress. But they made it through the checkpoint without incident, and that night he and his friend slept in his aunt and uncle's home in West Berlin. It was the first night of his life he'd been in a democratic country.

"What made you decide to leave then?" Jasmine asked him.

"I just didn't see a happy future for myself in the GDR," Uwe said. "And there was no way to know the wall would come down in a couple of years. No one even dreamed about that. I was young, restless, no family that depended on me. Why wait? I still like the teachings of Karl Marx. It's just that the system doesn't work."

"You must have been relieved when you heard he made it," Jasmine said to me.

"Honestly? I was mad. I mean, he was still my friend, and I was glad he wasn't hurt. But I didn't support his defection, because from my point of view, he betrayed our country. He betrayed our beliefs. That's how I saw it. I felt betrayed, as well."

"I don't get it," Jasmine said.

"He went to school, studied, and it was all free. He didn't have to pay for it. That was the way it was in our country. And once his education was done, my feeling was he should have felt an obligation to give back to society. Instead, he left. He never gave back. That's how I saw it. His point of view, of course, was different. And now that I've lived in a free country, in a democracy, I agree with him. But at that point in time, I didn't know. I'd grown up in the GDR, in my closed little sports world, not really knowing what was going on outside."

"But you'd been outside. You'd seen the way things were in the West."

"You have to remember I was very much a product of our system. I owed so much to it. And I didn't know what it meant to be free. My parents never complained to me about it. I don't even know if they noticed it. Their generation didn't show their emotions. They'd gone through so much. My father was born in 1938 and my mother in 1936, so they were seven and nine years old at the end of the war, when things were really terrible. They were just children, and they had to leave their homes to escape the fighting and pull their possessions behind them in a wagon. They were hungry and cold and homeless. And they never complained. I've never heard them complain once. My mother used to tell me about going to the dentist, where she had to choose between having a tooth pulled after using a painkiller or saving money by just having it pulled out without painkiller. She'd always choose to save the money. I can't believe that. I need a shot if a dentist just looks at my teeth. Still, I've never heard either one of them complain. I've always admired that. That's the way I grew up."

"Unbelievable," Jasmine said.

"And, you know, the GDR wasn't such a bad place for us. My father was a farmer. My mother was a physical therapist at a hospital. Those are not professions that pay a lot of money. If I'd grown up in America, or anywhere in the West, I'd never have been able to be a skater. There it comes down to whether you can afford the coach, afford the private tutor, afford to pay for the skates and the dresses and time on the ice. Especially a world-class coach like Frau Müller. I never would have been a skater if I'd grown up outside the GDR."

"But afterward? Once you'd seen the world and won the two gold medals and paid back the system that groomed you, you never wanted to defect?" she asked.

"I could have done it. I could have defected. I had offers to go to the West and make a lot of money. But that was never a temptation for me, because I didn't want to risk never seeing my parents and my friends again. That would have broken my heart. Uwe just went for it. He went for his dream. That's what he wanted. That was his passion. He decided he wasn't going to stay in this country and grow old here. He decided he was going to see the world. He planned it and left, and even if he felt some sadness and loneliness at times, he never regretted it. He went to medical school in Vienna and became an orthopedist. And luckily for him, the wall came down two years later. But what if it had taken ten or fifteen years? All that time without seeing your family. I couldn't imagine it."

"Just as I couldn't imagine staying," Uwe said.

"Still, he was my friend, and he knew he was my friend," I

said. "So when he had a chance to reconnect with me after he'd defected, he did it. I was skating in a show in Dortmund, and he came backstage to greet me. It was a complete surprise, and I was really happy to see him again. I didn't judge him. He was somebody from my past, which was precious to me. Still, when I came home I couldn't tell anyone I'd seen him. It had to be secret."

"And he didn't try to talk you into defecting, too?" Jasmine asked.

"I'd already had a chance to see the world, because I was an athlete," I said. "I'd traveled, even if it was usually for competitions. It wasn't quite the same as being a tourist and seeing the sights, because I was always under pressure to bring a gold medal home. But I always squeezed in some sightseeing. And still I was always happy to come back home. I had my chances to defect, but not knowing what might happen to my parents and my friends . . . I just couldn't do it. Uwe could."

"And you didn't care about the money? That you might have been giving up a fortune by staying in the GDR?"

"Honestly, when I was twenty I never thought about having a professional career in skating, because there was no such thing in my country. The best I could hope for was becoming a coach, like Frau Müller. I only thought about the season I was in. I was an athlete in my heart, not my head. It was only later I became a businesswoman. Money or fame can't be your motivation to get to the top in athletics. That's not what you torture yourself for. It has to be for something bigger than dollar signs. You suffer. It hurts. You cry. Why? It has to be: Someday, I'll be the best. Not someday I'll get a big paycheck. That will never work. There's just something on the inside that burns, an unquenchable desire to be the best in your field. That's the only real motivation.

There are easier ways to make a lot of money than by being an athlete. There are easier ways to achieve fame. If you're an athlete the only question you have to ask yourself is: Do I want to be the best? And what do I have to do for that to happen?"

"Regardless of the consequences? Regardless of who you hurt or leave behind?" Jasmine asked pointedly.

"Every decision you make involves consequences," I said to her. "Following your dreams means taking risks. For me, I had to give up things to become a champion skater. For Uwe, he did the same to defect to the West."

She thought about that. It was exactly what we'd been talking about ever since she'd arrived in Berlin: the high cost of following your dreams.

12

Lillehammer Olympics, 1994

In the morning when I went in to wake Jasmine, she was packing her bag.

"Leaving today?" I asked.

"You've been so great. I can't impose any longer. I really can't. But thank you for everything. You've been a big help whether you know it or not."

"Have I? I'm glad."

"You'd be a wonderful mom."

I smiled. "I would keep you in a heartbeat." I noticed a pair of skates on the top of her bag. "You brought your skates. I should have asked. You could have skated with me yesterday."

"I just threw them in. I much preferred watching you."

"What about today? I have a meeting this morning, but I have ice at the rink from eleven to twelve. There are just four of us who use it. You could join us. Please do."

She smiled at me. "Maybe I should. You can give me some pointers."

"No pointers. Frau Müller won't be there. We'll just skate."

"It would be fun."

"I think so, too."

"Then I have to go visit my friend. She was expecting me yesterday," Jasmine said.

"As you wish. And have you decided what you're going to do as far as your skating goes?"

"I know I'll keep skating. I mean, duh. I love it. Whether I go to America to train or not, stay tuned. As you said, it's not a decision I have to make today. Soon, though. I want to talk to my mother more about it, to try to understand why she wants me to go so badly. I'm going to tell her some of your thoughts. And I've got to talk to my Dad. He's not at home anymore, and he's never, you know, really taken this as seriously as everyone else. I think that must somehow have rubbed off on me. It's not like he's against my skating, but he keeps waiting for me to outgrow it. Go to college. To start, I don't know, my real life. I don't think he sees that this is my real life. That I wouldn't be me without skating. I have to make him understand that, because his support means a lot to me."

"As it should."

"Of course I have to discuss it more with Bernard." She arched her eyebrows. "Not looking forward to that."

"Hmm."

"And I've got to do some soul-searching. Try to figure out what's really inside of me. I mean, is it in me to have the sort of passion for the sport that you do? I gotta figure that out."

"But remember, sweetie, I wasn't the same at sixteen as I am now. That's when I was running to the candy store instead of training."

"And pinching your cheeks to give them color when you returned."

I laughed. "And I never got caught!"

"I love that. Can you show me that last scrapbook on the Lillehammer Olympics? Do you have time?"

"Come on. It won't take long, and it always brings back fond memories."

She followed me to my office, where the scrapbooks were still stacked on the floor. I knelt down and found the one that began in 1993. "I'd turned professional, you know. I'd been ineligible for the 1992 Albertville Games, but then the ISU—the International Skating Union—changed their eligibility rules and opened up the 1994 Olympics to the pros, as long as you declared your intention to be reinstated by January 1993. It was a funny period. The skaters were all making money, so it wasn't a question of professionals and amateurs. It was all about being eligible or ineligible for the Olympics. And that was determined by the ISU. To be eligible you had to compete solely in ISU-sanctioned events. So it was a power play, really, all about money and control. Anyway, some of us took advantage of the chance to return to the Olympics and asked to be reinstated. Jayne Torvill and Christopher Dean. Brian Boitano. Ekaterina Gordeeva and Sergei Grinkov. And me."

"What was there to lose?"

"Actually, you could hurt your reputation. A lot of people in Germany thought I was just doing it to get back in the news. I'd been spending most of my time touring in the States, since there weren't any skating shows in Germany, so they thought my comeback was phony. They thought I was just doing it for the attention, and I'd probably pull out at the very end so as not to embarrass myself. If my comeback was terrible, if I didn't make the German national team, for example, it would have been damaging to my professional career. That was the risk. I was twenty-seven. I wasn't in competitive shape. I hadn't been skating three to four hours a day, as you need to do for the Olympics. I still had my triple toe and triple salchow, but I had to try to get back my triple loop. The younger skaters could do more triples, but luckily figure skating has more than just triple jumps to it."

"Why did you come back, then? Did you think you could win?"

I laughed. "No. I knew I had no chance. But I wanted the challenge. I wanted to prove that, even though I was twenty-seven, I was still among the best in the world. Not the best, but one of a handful of the best. That, athletically, I wasn't 'an old broad.' Nobody was going to tell me: You're twenty-seven. You're too old. You have to find this out for yourself. Plus, the timing was right. Brian and I had just lost our *skating* tour, which we'd done the last three years. It had just started to break even when Bill Graham, the promoter, died in a helicopter crash. The coproducer sold it to IMG—International Management Group—in the fall of 1992. Even though Brian and I had started it, we didn't own anything. We were just artists. So that was my first lesson in capitalism. You can't just be the artist. You have to own something, too. So all of a sudden, for the first time since the wall came down, I had to make a conscious decision: Where am I going with my career? I wasn't just going with the flow. I'd never been forced to sit down and think about that. I'd just gone from one thing to the next, from the tour to pro competitions to planning the next tour. Now I had to ask myself: Do I want a new challenge or to go back to touring for somebody else?"

"And you chose the challenge."

"I decided I didn't want the easy way. I'd take that challenge. I was afraid I might fail, but I'm stubborn, and if I got to the Olympics, I'd have accomplished all that I'd hoped for. It didn't really matter how I did once I got there. The point was to make it to Lillehammer."

"And Frau Müller ? What did she think?"

"She hadn't coached me in four years. But I called her. I told her what I wanted to do, but only on the condition that she train me. If she'd told me it was a waste of time, that she wouldn't do it, I wouldn't have come back."

"And she was psyched."

"She respected that I wanted to come back. It was a different relationship now, more like woman to woman versus coach to athlete. It was more a relationship built on respect for each other. She knew I'd work hard. She knew I wasn't coming back to embarrass myself. And I had another motivation as well, one that she completely understood. I wanted to skate a tribute to Sarajevo, which was in the middle of a terrible civil war. That, of course, was where I'd won my first gold medal. I wanted to skate to Pete Seeger's song "Where Have All the Flowers Gone" at the Olympics. That was the main reason I went back and worked as hard as I did. I didn't want to get my triple jumps back so I could be competitive and win another medal. I got the triples back so I could show that program to the Olympics audience. It was all about that song and the message I wanted to bring across. Look, we can't forget about Sarajevo, where ten years ago the Olympics were held and the whole world came together in peace. Where a sports competition brought people of different traditions, cultures, and religions together from all over the world. And then all of a sudden this terrible war erupts between Christians and Muslims, and family and friends start killing each other. It was horrifying to hear those stories. And to me it was very personal. The arena where I skated was destroyed. There was a brand new cemetery outside it. It was heartbreaking, because the people of Sarajevo had been all-embracing, so welcoming as Olympic hosts. And now it was torn apart by war, right in the heart of Europe, and it seemed like the rest of the world was watching, paralyzed. At the time, my motivation was to send a message out to people all over the world, using television and the Olympic stage, to not forget about Sarajevo."

"I remember that program. I think I was six years old, but I remember my mother watching it and crying. It made her cry."

"That's what our sport can do, Jasmine. That's the magic. I don't want to sound immodest, but I thought I could bring something to Olympic skating that had been missing. I thought I could bring passion to the sport. I know that when I go to a skating competition, I want to be impressed. I want to sit there and be touched. That's what I think skating should be. Someone running around from jump to jump with a lot of connecting steps doesn't impress me. It doesn't make me care. There are brilliant skaters who are just out there doing a job. There's a wall around them. They don't let the audience participate. They don't let them see into their hearts. I want to see beauty and characters and athleticism and to get emotionally involved when I watch skating. I want to get goose bumps."

"I'm getting goose bumps just listening to you talk about it," Jasmine said.

"There are only a few who can do that for me. Brian Boitano, Brian Orser, and Kurt Browning. Kristi Yamaguchi has done that for me. Alexei Yagudin at the 2002 Olympics. You watched his free program and you knew there was someone making history. He was completely involved in it in his heart. Evgeny Plushenko. There's someone who just loves what he's doing. He can give me goose bumps every time. Tara Lipinski at the Nagano Olympics in 1998, who was so youthful, so fresh, so energetic . . . even though Michelle Kwan is a soulful skater, all of a sudden she looked tired beside her. And Sarah Hughes in Salt Lake City in 2002 had that same spark of innocence and freshness. But she lost it, you know, when she turned pro. It was so sad, but you could see Sarah had lost her love of the sport, lost that spark that had set her apart at the Olympics. She felt the burden of being the Olympic champion, I think. Her heart wasn't in it, and an audience can't be fooled. That joyful exuberance only works when you're young. Then, if you stay in skating, you have to grow from there. You shouldn't grow into something boring, but into something exciting and passionate and womanly. That's what I kept hearing, anyway, before Lillehammer. People kept telling me they were looking forward to my program because a real woman would be coming onto the ice. I mean, of course, Nancy Kerrigan was a woman on the ice as well. But she was different. She was more of a technical skater, a strong jumper. My artistic side was my best weapon. So I wanted to take that challenge, because I didn't want to look back with regret later on. I took the risk of failing. And the result was that I gained from it as a person, Jasmine. I took a great deal from the experience, and I won a lot of hearts, too. And I accomplished my biggest goal of getting people to think about what was happening in Sarajevo."

"Marlene Dietrich did the famous antiwar version of 'Where Have All the Flowers Gone,' right? Is that why you chose it?"

"She did it, yes, but it was the Joan Baez version that inspired me. I used to listen to that when I was a girl. So I called Pete Seeger to get his permission to use it, because in order to skate to 'Where Have All the Flowers Gone,' it had to be completely rearranged. I knew only Sandra Bezic could make it work. Only she could choreograph a competitive program out of a song like that. And it was quite a process. We took original explosion noises from the television coverage of the war in Sarajevo, when the bombs were going off and a helicopter was landing, and dubbed it into the sound track. And once we had the program finished, I knew that it was expressive and would move the audience. So I had to make the Olympics and show it to the world. Whatever I needed to get that done, that's what I would do. If it had been just a normal free program, with jumps and choreography, I don't think I'd have made the personal sacrifice."

Jasmine was flipping the pages of the scrapbook, looking at pictures of me in the dark red outfit I wore for the Lillehammer program. "It's beautiful. Your costume."

"I loved this costume, it was so simple."

"So how did it go?"

"People finally got the message I was serious. I completely removed myself from the public eye to train, and I wouldn't take any money from the German Skating Federation. I took care of all my expenses. I could have asked for funding, but I thought: 'That's ridiculous. Others need it more.' So finally the German media started getting curious about how I was doing, because no one had seen my programs.

"I finally showed it in public for the first time at an exhibition in Frankfurt. I hadn't told anyone what I'd be skating to. It was a secret. I remember it was my birthday, December 3, and there were sixty journalists attending. Sixty! That never happens for an exhibition. And I was so nervous. I knew I was in shape, but mentally, I wasn't prepared. Not yet. I'll tell you why.

"Over that summer I'd been writing my biography in Germany, and when I do something, I do it completely. I have to give myself to it 100 percent. So the manuscript of my biography kept going back and forth between the ghostwriter and me for weeks. That's where my head was. Physically, I was ready to skate, but mentally sometimes I wasn't on the ice. I'd get a chapter, read it, and then while I was on the ice getting ready to try my combination jump, a thought would come into my head. I'd interrupt my training and go to the boards to write the thought down, because I didn't want to lose it. Usually these thoughts were very personal. Some things I wanted left in the book, but some things I wanted taken out, because I just wasn't ready to share them. And there was a deadline approaching, since the publisher wanted the book to come out in time for Christmas, which is when everyone buys books. And we were behind schedule.

"So at the exhibition on my birthday, when I was unveiling my program for the first time, I fell on the first jump. After that, my program basically fell apart."

"Oh, God. I know that feeling."

"I'd been away from competition so long I'd lost the ability to really focus. I'd lost my competitive edge. It had been my strength, and I'd lost it. As an athlete you need continuity, or you just lose it. And I was also very, very nervous. I saw all the journalists and knew how seriously they were taking this exhibition—my comeback!—and, God, it was so bad. I was crying and so disappointed in myself. I came home totally crushed. Totally."

"I can't picture you ever being totally crushed."

"I was then. Like I told you before, I'm not a robot. But I still had two weeks time until Nationals. I knew I was in great shape. So Frau Müller told me, 'You've got to decide. You can concentrate on this, or not.' But she was supportive. She knew I had all my jumps back and that I was physically prepared. It was just a matter now of getting my head back together.

"So I called Elisabeth and told her: 'Forget the book. Just forget it. I won't work on it until after the Nationals are done, between Christmas and New Year's Day. Not before.' So of course the publishing house went crazy, totally losing it, because now they'd miss the Christmas season. But I told Elisabeth I didn't care. They could have their advance back. I'd pay for their losses out of my own pocket, if that's what they wanted. They were losing money, but I was in danger of losing my reputation. And that's what mattered to me. I got my priorities right. And Elisabeth was great. She said: 'If this is what you have to do, then that's what we'll do.' And even the publishers went along with it, reluctantly. They thought I was killing them, but what were they going to do?

"Two weeks later I went to Nationals, and I did incredibly, I must say. I did a perfect short program—I was skating to the sound track from *Robin Hood*—and my free program was good, too. I did four triples, leaving out my triple loop, which I really hadn't done since 1988. But I made a mistake on my last double axel. Afterward, a lot of people said I should have been national champion, but Tanja Szewczenko did more jumps, and she won. She was coached by Peter Meier at that time. Maybe you've seen her with him."

"I've met her," Jasmine said.

"Anyway, there were some politics involved in the judging, since she was from Dortmund and most of the judges were West German. I'm not saying Tanja didn't deserve it. But as is typical in figure skating, afterward a number of people told me I should have won. It wasn't easy to be from the GDR at that time if you were an athlete or coach. For example, the German Skating Federation completely ignored Frau Müller after the wall came down. They didn't hire her to coach any of the top skaters, and she was the best in the world. Big mistake. Big, big mistake. It was like: We're the winners, and now we'll put you East Germans in your place. But it didn't really matter as far as the Olympics went, since the top three places at Nationals all went to the European championships, and the Olympic team would be selected by the top two German skaters from that. So really, the 1993 Nationals was a big triumph for both Frau Müller and me, especially after I'd messed up so badly two weeks earlier. People gave me a lot of credit for pulling myself back together. Then between Christmas and New Year's I finished editing my biography."

"So was the third Olympics different from the first two?"

"Oh, yes. I was able to celebrate it the way I'd always wanted. I rented a big house in Lillehammer, which was like this fairy-tale dreamland covered with snow, and my whole family was there: my brother, his girlfriend, my parents, Elisabeth, Uwe, and other friends. I think there were twelve people staying there. I wanted those who meant most to me in life to experience the event that meant most to me, the Olympic Games. None of them had ever gone before. They loved it, but I wasn't able to share their adventures because I was staying in the Olympic Village. It was important to me, because I wanted to be part of the team. I didn't want to be a party pooper. I wanted to watch the other athletes compete and really celebrate the Olympics. So I went to watch speed skating and a few other events. Then at night I'd go to the house I'd rented to have dinner with my family and friends. I cherished that time.

"It was a crazy year, with all the media frenzy surrounding Tonya Harding and Nancy Kerrigan. It was just nuts. You may have been too young to remember, Jasmine, but the husband of Tonya Harding hired some thug to break Nancy's kneecaps with a lead pipe, because Tonya couldn't beat her on the ice. The attack took place during a practice at the U.S. Nationals, and it was front-page news for weeks. Tonya, I would assume, knew about it beforehand. She always denied it, but that's what her husband said—that she was in on planning the attack. So there was this big scandal in America, and it created so much interest in the sport that it lasted all through the 1990s. People who didn't know anything about skating would tune in to see if there was more action going on, and there was an FBI investigation, and a lawsuit to keep Tonya on the U.S. Olympic team. In the end a lot of those people just fell in love with the sport. I felt very sorry for Nancy. She was trapped in the middle of this media circus, and after her knee healed she just wanted to move on. We eventually became very good friends. She's really a warm and giving person, but during that whole crazy scene she got distant from people, and her image really suffered."

"And what was Tonya Harding like?"

"Tonya," I chuckled ruefully. "She was an impressive athlete, I must say. Her jumps were so high. She was very talented, except not in the head. Really, I don't care two cents about her."

Jasmine just laughed.

"There I was watching this craziness in Lillehammer," I said, "and I felt like being a role model for all of them. I had two gold medals already, and my purpose in being there was different than it had been in my first two Olympics. I felt at ease with it. It was so nice not to worry about fighting for the gold. I kept telling myself I had no chance, to remove the pressure."

"And then something strange happened. I came in sixth in the short program. I did so well I started thinking: 'I could have been fourth, or even third.' Because Oksana Baiul made an obvious mistake, but the judges still put her ahead of me, even though I skated clean and she two-footed her combination jump."

"Is this you in the tights?" Jasmine asked, pointing to a photograph of me in my Robin Hood costume.

"That's me. Even though it was technically against the rules, I skated in tights, because I refused to play Robin Hood running through the forest in a skirt. The program came across so well I ended up in the last group of the free skate. Which was not at all what I'd expected. And I was skating last. I used to like skating last. It was my favorite position. But not that night. The truth is, I was conflicted because I knew I couldn't do what the other girls could do technically. But I hadn't come there to win."

"So were you more nervous than usual?"

"Not only that, but we had trouble getting tickets for my family and friends. I didn't even know if my parents were going to be in the building, and if they weren't, I really didn't want to perform. But as it turned out, Uwe bought twelve tickets on the black market, and they were all sitting together, and during the warm-ups I looked around and looked around, trying to find them. Uwe saw that, and he told them all to stand up and start screaming. They'd actually brought a bench into the arena, and they were all standing on it like a bunch of chickens. I was so relieved to find them. But I was still so nervous to be skating last."

"It's so hard," she said, turning the page. "You have such a long wait."

"Anyway," I sighed, "it didn't work out the way I'd hoped. I think what happened was at the last moment I got competitive. Which I shouldn't have. It was a time to go out and enjoy myself, like I do now when I skate in a show. I was in the place I wanted to be, performing this special program that I wanted to share with the world. And all of a sudden I got my competitive heart back. For this one time, that was wrong, because I tried to do more than I was capable of doing. You have to know your limitations. I wasn't capable of doing five triples in that program. The plan was to do four. But if I wanted to medal, I had to do five.

"I remember when I was getting ready to go on, Oksana was coming off the ice. She skated two skaters before me. And she started to have what looked like a nervous breakdown. She was sobbing uncontrollably. I realized later it was because she had won, but I was sitting there thinking, God, what's going on with her? There's a sixteen-year-old crying, and I'm thinking about her, when in a minute it was going to be my turn to skate. In the past I'd have blocked all that out, but I didn't want to focus on my nervousness. So I was taking in everything around me, which was weird and even more unsettling.

"Anyway, I went out and did my best, but I made a few mistakes. Still, the audience went crazy and jumped up and gave me a standing ovation. Everyone was touched by it, which is what people remember now. They remember the overall performance, not the mistakes. Afterward you could see me mouthing the words: 'I'm sorry.' I kept repeating that during this amazing reception by the audience. But in my heart I wasn't happy, because my original plan had been thrown into the shadows by my athletic heart, which all of a sudden told me: 'You have a chance for a medal. You can win a medal!' It was so frickin' stupid. But that was how I was brought up: to be an athlete. I'd always been taught to go to an event to win, not just to be a participant.

"It took me a long time to get over it, however. Even now, I feel like I failed. Which makes me understand better how terrible it must be for Rosalynn Sumners and Debi Thomas, who only had one Olympic experience and failed. It was hard. I came to Lillehammer with an idea I wanted to share, and I did that. At the same time it's the Olympics! I'm an athlete. I shouldn't just be an artist. So the athlete in me took over, when what I should have been concentrating on, pure and simple, was artistry. Maybe the athletic side would have clicked into gear, if I'd done that, as it had in the short program. That was my secret later on. I discovered if I didn't think too much about the jumps, if I became absorbed in my program, the jumps would happen. Like magic, they'd be there. But if I was too eager to land them, it wouldn't work."

"Maybe I should try that secret," Jasmine said.

"I recommend it. In practice, concentrate on landing your jumps. But in competition, lose yourself in your performance."

"I like that." She closed the scrapbook.

"I have my meeting to go to now. But I'll meet you at the rink, okay?" I scribbled the address on a piece of paper. "Take a taxi. Do you have money?"

She laughed. "Of course. Go on. I'll see you there."

"If I'm late, just go on the ice without me. Don't wait, okay?"

"Okay."

I waved good-bye and dashed down the stairs. Even after all those years, it still surprised me that I felt a twinge of regret when remembering Lillehammer, my last Olympic Games.

13
Good-bye

My meeting ran late, which often happens when you're dealing
with potential business partners. All you can do is smile and
make the best of it. I wasn't going to be on time for my skating
session with Jasmine, but I was driving as fast as I could to get
there before it ended at noon. That's the problem with owning
your own show and being your own boss: You can't take short-
cuts. It's your reputation at stake. If it comes out badly, there's
no one to blame but yourself. The struggle for me is to reconcile
what I want as an artist—this and this and this, everything!—and
what we can afford as a company. Elisabeth often spends time
trying to find more financing, but we've learned that sometimes
you have to make do with what you've got.

The traffic in Berlin that morning was terrible, and it soon
became clear I wouldn't be at the rink in time to skate. I still

wanted to watch Jasmine, to see how she looked on the ice. Not just to watch her jumps and spins and stroking, but to see whether her heart was in it. That's what I needed to find out. Whether skating gave her the joy that it always brought me.

That, more than anything else, has been why it's been so hard to say good-bye to performing. I still love it, and I know whatever comes next in my life will not be as stimulating or personally gratifying as my skating career has been. How could it be? In what other field could I know it was me who created the magic for people, only me, using the ice and the music? Not me and fifteen other people with whom I was working. It's like telling a poet he can no longer write poems. Move on. Try painting, instead. Try to teach. This is what makes it so hard.

Still, I know the end isn't far away. I've always gone season to season, never planning too far ahead. But my body is telling me now, 'Maybe one more season,' and I'm old enough to listen. Physically, it's so demanding. It's getting too hard to train the three or four hours a day it takes to get myself in shape every year. And you want to leave your audience when they still think to themselves: "I will miss her."

There will be something else, some other pursuit to pique my interest. I'm not struggling with what to do next in my life. I always have good instincts, and I follow them. I listen to my gut, as Americans like to say. A friend once asked me what I thought I'd have been if I'd been born in America, what profession, and I told him I probably wouldn't have been a skater. I couldn't have afforded it. Maybe I'd have been a performer of some kind; an actress, perhaps. But he thought I'd have been a businesswoman. He says I have a good business mind.

It's not instinct. I didn't know a thing about business when I was young, so it can't be instinct. If I'm successful at business, it's because I've learned from the people around me. I'm good at surrounding myself with talented people, and at listening to them. Get a good team together, and trust them to bring your visions to life. In the past, the team I trusted was my coach, my athletic trainer, my choreographer, my teachers, and, of course, my parents. Now it's different, but it's still a team. Lea Ann Miller, whom I've worked with for many years, is my choreographer and the director of my shows. I trust her, and she's become a very close friend of mine. There's my physical therapist and hair stylist and publicist and manager, all of whom play essential roles. And my parents are there for me still. I've seen athletes who only trust their parents or their coaches. They never move on. They're stuck in their own little world. I've tried to expand my world. I still embrace challenges. Elisabeth can talk me into things she thinks will be good down the road, because she thinks several steps ahead, and I'm not looking that far ahead until she explains it. I'm good at admitting my weaknesses. That's my business mind. I can delegate. I'm not someone who believes I can do it alone.

We try to plan as far ahead as possible. That way we're able to build up a network. And now that I'm doing some of my own productions, I know how important it is to honor your commitments. So if I say I'll appear somewhere, or do something, I'll follow through unless both my feet are broken. Because I know what's involved for the people on the other end. Not everyone is like that, and once you burn bridges behind you, it's very difficult to build those bridges back up. What goes around, comes around. One of my favorite sayings is: You meet people twice. Once, on the way up, and a second time on the way back down. That's how I try to live my life.

So when I look to the future, a future when I'm no longer

skating, I have a calm feeling. Some athletes fall into a very deep hole after their careers end. They don't know what to do with their lives. Even if they have plenty of money, they need to channel their energy somewhere. All they've done is sports, and the beauty of sports is that whatever success you achieve is the result of talent and hard work. Maybe a little bit of luck. You have control over it. In other professions, it's how you're marketed, who you know, how well you're perceived by people in a position of power. It isn't necessarily talent. You need lots of luck. You need to be in the right place at the right time. Athletes who go into another field at the end of their careers have to accept that they won't be the best. They'll be starting over from scratch, and other people their age will be far ahead of them in experience. It's as if they've just left school. It's understandable to be afraid of that. You hear lots of stories of musicians or actors or athletes who make a lot of money when they're young. Eventually they burn through it all and end up with nothing left. It's sad. Fame and fortune at a young age can prove to be a bargain with Faust.

All these thoughts were running through my head, when suddenly I saw the ice rink ahead. A delivery truck beside me had me trapped in the center lane, and the driver ignored my turn signal and wouldn't let me over. I had to slam on the brakes at the last second and cut across two lanes of traffic to make the turn into the parking lot. When I looked at my watch, I saw it was quarter to twelve. I had fifteen minutes to watch Jasmine skate.

There's a glass wall on one side of the rink, and I stood behind it so as not to distract her. Jasmine was wearing a one-piece leotard, all black, which complimented what was, to me, a perfect figure for a figure skater, lithe and svelte without appearing skinny. She stroked with real strength and moved with speed across the ice. I was struck again by her natural beauty. Jasmine had this freshness about her, a bright air of innocence that filled the rink and would definitely help her with the judges. She was not a woman on the ice at all, but a bud of a girl with all of her future before her.

It made me feel sentimental. I thought back on what it was like when I was young, skating with Brian Boitano on our first projects, with Brian Orser and Rosalynn Sumners on tour. I thought about the times when all my friends had their futures ahead of them. My generation of skaters was lucky. We had longevity that the young stars don't really have today. People now are already forgetting about Tara Lipinski, and even Sarah Hughes. They're just young girls, here today and then they're gone. Before we've even gotten to know them, they move on and we're left to wonder: Where's the next one? I was able to skate in three Olympics. I feel I had a chance to burn myself into people's hearts.

Even now, inside I still feel like that budding girl I was watching on the ice. That's what happens when you follow your passion. It keeps you young. When I thought of myself, I still thought of that girl of seventeen. Hopeful. Ambitious. Too focused on the next step to be scared. It was no problem at all to remember the giddy feeling of skating on a clean sheet of ice, my hair blowing behind, the air in my face imparting the feeling of speed, the smiling eyes of boys turned in my direction. It's one of the purest joys I've ever known—skating. It makes me sad to think of leaving it behind.

But this is life. We grow or we die, like the trees. It's in my nature to discover other passions. And as I watched Jasmine skate, I began to hope she might have been rediscovering hers.

From our few days together I hoped she would remember one thing: You can't have it all. Somewhere you must make a sacrifice. You have to give something up in order to gain anything meaningful. It makes no sense to go through life saying: 'If I do this, I could lose that.' Better to ask yourself, 'If I do this, what might I gain?'

There's no real answer to that. You can't know what you have to gain. Not the way you know what you're giving up (the dance; the party; the weekend at the ski lodge). Life takes you on a path, and who knows where that path will lead? The possibilities for what lie ahead are endless. Endless. At sixteen, you can't imagine what might lie ahead in ten years if you try to reach your dream. It could be anything. Or nothing. But when you're young and you're fortunate to have found your passion, go for it. Don't be stifled by the fear of failure. Don't worry that there are no guarantees. Make the first step. Embrace the future. Embrace the possibilities that the future holds.

Do it for yourself, not anyone else. If somebody you love wants you to stay home and be with him, you have to decide if that's what you want. If you want it, then do it. But don't do it because he wants it, or later on you'll point the finger and blame him for not following your heart. For sacrificing your dreams. You should always point the finger at yourself. You made the decision, not him. That's what I believe about relationships, too. Your partner isn't responsible for your happiness. You're responsible. Don't expect somebody else to make you happy. Don't say to your partner: 'But you didn't make me happy.' That's not right. The happiness should come from you.

Don't even do it for your parents. You can't go through life trying to please them, because in the final analysis, as much as they love you, it's your life. Those are your drawers to fill with memories. No one else will be able to open them to see if they hold wonderful memories or not.

I once read something about the actor Benicio Del Toro, who starred in *Traffic*. His parents wanted him to go to a regular school and study, so he'd have a good future. He told them that's what he was doing. Instead, he enrolled in acting school and never let them know. They never found out until he won an Oscar for best supporting actor. Now, of course, they're proud of him. But he followed his passion, his heart. His parents wanted what was best for him, but he didn't follow their advice, and it worked out, because once you believe you're destined for something and will do anything to get better at it, you'll be the best. You'll work endless hours. You won't be lazy. Somehow, somewhere, sometime, your self-belief will pay off, and you'll get a chance to show what you can do. And your parents will respect you for following your own path, even if it's not the path they'd hoped for. It's like the lesson I learned when I moved into my own apartment when I was nineteen: You can rebel from your parents without rejecting them. As long as they see you're working and have a purpose in life, they'll understand. Sometimes you have to go your own way in order to move forward in life.

All these things I was thinking while watching Jasmine skate. The music that was playing was Sarah McLachlan's "Angel," which is a lovely, haunting ballad, and she was skating to it dreamily, languidly, as if she alone could hear the soft, sad tune. It was pleasant to watch her, but she was uninspired. The song ended, and Jasmine took a short rest along the boards. She was alone on the ice. Then a new song came over the speaker, one I hadn't heard before. She listened for a few bars, then moved to the center, nodding her head as she went. Then it happened. I saw what I'd been hoping to see.

The recording was by an artist I didn't recognize. He was playing what I can only describe as a reggae version of "Over the Rainbow." It wasn't the wistful, longing lullaby that Judy Garland sang in *The Wizard of Oz*, but an off-tempo, upbeat version, eminently danceable. Certainly Jasmine found she could dance to it. Her entire body language changed as she invented her own choreography. The beat seemed to free her, and she lost her inhibitions. She invented a little sideways dance move, first tap-dancing left, then sliding back to the right, then back to the left again with a funny juke, and onward down the ice.

I found myself tapping my foot and swaying to the reggae beat. The singer accompanied himself with a simple acoustic instrument. Perhaps it was a ukulele. I wasn't sure. But it was fun. And he sung with a sweet Caribbean accent, Jamaican or Bahamian . . . "Why then oh why can't I?"

I stepped through the glass door, so I was in the arena with her. Jasmine was spinning now, her head thrown back, and she was smiling, beaming at the ceiling. She was in a zone of her own. I was invisible to her. The world was invisible. She looked to me like the physical embodiment of youth.

This is what I've loved about our sport. It's transporting in the simplest, purest way. You don't have to be in the Olympics. You don't have to stand on the podium. A sheet of ice, a song, a skater, a practice. They come together, and without a choreographer, without a coach, even, what's created can move someone to remembering a special place in her youth. This is the journey that makes all the work worthwhile. I was seeing it unfold right before my eyes.

The rich, Belafonte-like tenor phrased "The dreams that you dare to dream really do come true," as Jasmine continued her spin, face upturned, her hair flying behind her. Her toe wasn't pointed quite right, but I wouldn't even have wanted her to change that. I'd rather see a skater's temperament and spirit on the ice than clean, perfect lines. Jasmine's eyes were closed as her arms reached skyward, performing a sort of snakelike dance above the breathtaking layback position. I felt a grin spread over my face, and as she came to a stop with the closing bars of the melody—"Why oh why oh why oh why can't I"—I felt the tears come into my eyes. She'd surprised me. She'd exposed something of her soul to me just then. What I'd seen was pure, unbridled joy.

It was then she caught my eye. I clasped my hands together beneath my chin and nodded. One time. Only that. I suppose she could see my smile, but it was the only communication we would share before we parted. It was our good-bye.

I realized then that it didn't matter what she did next. Jasmine would be all right. She had passion; that much was clear. The important thing was for her to follow it wherever it might lead, to pursue it with the fervor of someone afraid of losing something dear. What a precious gift it is to have talent and passion, both. It didn't ultimately matter if she went to America to train or to a simple life back home in the town in which she was raised. Or even if she decided to give up skating and go to college. It didn't matter if she ever became a champion. She'd discovered something a lot of people have never found. She discovered the magic's in the journey.

It's what gives shape and purpose to our lives. It's what makes us who we are. And, as I'm about to learn again—because this journey never ends—it determines what one day we might be.

THE END

PUBLICAFFAIRS is a publishing house founded in 1997. It is a tribute to the standards, values, and flair of three persons who have served as mentors to countless reporters, writers, editors, and book people of all kinds, including me.

I. F. STONE, proprietor of *I. F. Stone's Weekly*, combined a commitment to the First Amendment with entrepreneurial zeal and reporting skill and became one of the great independent journalists in American history. At the age of eighty, Izzy published *The Trial of Socrates*, which was a national bestseller. He wrote the book after he taught himself ancient Greek.

BENJAMIN C. BRADLEE was for nearly thirty years the charismatic editorial leader of *The Washington Post*. It was Ben who gave the *Post* the range and courage to pursue such historic issues as Watergate. He supported his reporters with a tenacity that made them fearless, and it is no accident that so many became authors of influential, best-selling books.

ROBERT L. BERNSTEIN, the chief executive of Random House for more than a quarter century, guided one of the nation's premier publishing houses. Bob was personally responsible for many books of political dissent and argument that challenged tyranny around the globe. He is also the founder and was the longtime chair of Human Rights Watch, one of the most respected human rights organizations in the world.

·　　　·　　　·

For fifty years, the banner of Public Affairs Press was carried by its owner Morris B. Schnapper, who published Gandhi, Nasser, Toynbee, Truman, and about 1,500 other authors. In 1983 Schnapper was described by *The Washington Post* as "a redoubtable gadfly." His legacy will endure in the books to come.

Peter Osnos, *Publisher*